Praise for *Compassion*

An in-depth and engaging study of compassion that will inspire a heartfelt life.

—Martine Batchelor, author of *Meditation for Life*
and *The Path of Compassion*

Compassion is an invaluable help for anyone who wants to make this a better world, both for others and in one's heart. Guiding us with clarity, vision, and lovingkindness, Christina Fieldman reveals a path that takes us beyond sorrow and frustration to genuine freedom.

—Sharon Salzberg, author of *Lovingkindness*

This informative and wide-ranging exploration of the practice of compassion will help open your eyes to the world's pain in such a way that you can learn to respond to it from the depths of your heart.

—Stephen Batchelor, author of *Buddhism Without Beliefs*
and *Living with the Devil*

Christina Feldman's book inspires us with the importance of practicing compassion. And what could be more important than having compassion for self and others in the tumultuous world in which we live? Savor this book slowly. To do so will change your life.

—Judith Hanson Lasater, Ph.D., P.T.,
author of *30 Essential Yoga Poses*

COMPASSION

By Christina Feldman

Silence: How to Find Inner Peace in a Busy World (2003)

Woman Awake: Women Practicing Buddhism (2005)

Compassion: Listening to the Cries of the World (2005)

COMPASSION

LISTENING TO THE CRIES OF THE WORLD

CHRISTINA FELDMAN

Shambhala • Boulder • 2005

Shambhala Publications, Inc.
4720 Walnut Street
Boulder, Colorado 80301
www.shambhala.com

A Rodmell Press book

Cover images: Head of Buddha in the Hadda style. The Buddhist art of the Hadda area is a unique fusion of Greco-Roman and local styles. Frontal view, 4th century CE, 35 cm high. Coll. Theresa McCollough, London, Great Britain. Photo: Werner Forman/ Art Resource, NY Tapestry conceived and composed by Gopa & Ted2, Inc. Author photograph by Libby Vigeon.

Permissions appear on page 159.

9 8 7 6 5 4 3 2

Printed in the United States of America

♾ This edition is printed on acid-free paper that meets the American National Standards Institute Z39.48 Standard.
♻ Shambhala Publications makes every effort to print on recycled paper. For more information please visit www.shambhala.com.
Distributed in the United States by Penguin Random House LLC and in Canada by Random House of Canada Ltd

Editor: Holly Hammond   Indexer: Ty Koontz
Project Director: Linda Cogozzo   Text Design: Gopa & Ted2, Inc.
Text set in Joanna 11/16

Library of Congress Cataloging-in-Publication Data

Feldman, Christina.
Compassion: listening to the cries of the world/Christina Feldman.—1st ed.
p. cm.
Includes index.
ISBN 978-1-930485-11-2 (pbk.: alk. paper)
1. Compassion—Religious aspects—Buddhism. 2. Religious life—Buddhism. I. Title.
BQ4360.F45 2005
294.3'5677—dc22
2005012931

Contents

Acknowledgments

M Y OWN JOURNEY to understanding the nature of compassion began in the early 1970s, when I lived among a community of Tibetan refugees. Each day I saw people whose lives had been devastated and yet who lived without bitterness or hatred.

To my earliest teacher, Geshe Rabten, and to all of his teachers, I owe an immense debt of gratitude. His teachings on compassion as being the beginning and the end of the spiritual path touched me profoundly.

The many teachers I have had the privilege of listening to throughout the years echoed the same message. I bow to them all.

I am grateful to the many dharma friends and colleagues in my life, who have touched me with their compassion and their love of awakening. They inspire me, delight me, and move me with their dedication to contributing in whatever way they can to bring about the end of sorrow.

I am grateful to my family for their love and support.

No path and no book is brought to completion without a wide circle of support, inspiration, and care. My thanks to Rodmell Press and Linda Cogozzo, for their great attention to detail and their commitment to bringing this book into being.

Introduction

A YOUNG NUN was arrested at midnight and placed in a prison for the next six months. Twice a week she was taken from her cell, blindfolded, bound, and interrogated. Beaten and tortured, she said,

> To stay alive, I meditated on peace and nonviolence every possible moment that I could. I tried my hardest to think of His Holiness the Dalai Lama and of peace for all humankind. Again and again, I meditated on my prayers. I did not feel particularly sad or angry. If the police noticed my lips moving, they told me to stop or I would be punished further. So I whispered my prayers secretly, barely moving my lips at all.
>
> A group of us celebrated the Dalai Lama birthday in prison by singing traditional Tibetan songs. As punishment for this action, the Chinese guards put me in an ice house and removed my clothing for three days. Then the beatings resumed and they went on and on for weeks. My prayers for peace and nonviolence also went on and on, with even greater intensity.[1]

When we hear stories of unimaginable suffering that are met with remarkable human courage and compassion, we are often left feeling skeptical or bewildered. We may be tempted to see these people as saints, possessed of qualities and powers inaccessible to us. But stories of great suffering are often stories of ordinary people that have found greatness of heart. We must not romanticize or idealize compassion. It is born of our willingness to meet pain rather than to run from it. Sometimes, compassion emerges in the darkest moments of life, when all doors of escape are closed and our hearts have turned to stone.

The Dalai Lama once said, "If you want to know what compassion is, look deeply into the eyes of a mother as she cradles her sick and fevered child." The unconditional acceptance, patience, and forbearance you would find in her eyes are not unknown to any of us. The wish to bring pain to an end, to heal and be present for another person in their anguish are qualities we have all aspired to and embodied. You know the power of compassion. You have encountered moments when your walls of defense and resistance crumbled and profound compassion emerged, and your heart has been comforted and altered by the compassion, tenderness, and forgiveness you have received from others.

At every turn of life, we all face events and situations of pain and anguish that can at times feel unbearable, yet must be borne. The limits of our tolerance, forgiveness, and patience are constantly being tested. The images of cruelty and hatred delivered through newspapers and television sadden us and appall us in equal measure. As human beings, our capacity to experience pain is our common denominator. You may not personally find yourself in a perilous situation in which your life is endangered, yet pain and anguish are undeniable aspects of being alive. Every human journey has its stories of tragedy and loss, disappointment and fear. The experiences of frailty and pain in your body, the moments of emotional and psychological turmoil are inescapable. Colleagues may frustrate you, lovers betray you, children leave you, and you can't build walls powerful enough to protect you. Life cannot be controlled or predicted. In moments of pain, fear, anger, and the desire for self-protection are provoked to the surface. In those moments, you face a choice—your heart can close, your mind recoil, and your body contract, or you can dive deeply inward to find and nurture the balance, resilience, and courage that allow you to deepen and care.

Compassion is not a quality to be cultivated in isolation, aloof from life. It is easy to be compassionate from a distance, when your heart is undisturbed. When you are surrounded by those who love and care for you, when you have built a world where pain is repressed or ignored, you can easily immerse yourself in thoughts of love and tolerance. Yet that is a fragile world, built on foundations that will always crumble. Compassion speaks of the willingness to engage with tragedy, loss, and pain. Its domain is not only the world of those you love and care for, but equally the people who threaten you, the countless people you don't know, the homeless person you meet on the street, and the situations of anger and hatred you recoil from. It is here that you learn about the depths of tolerance and understanding that are possible for each one of us. It is here that you learn about dignity, meaning, and greatness of heart. As a rabbinic text encourages us, "in the places where there are no human beings, be one."

The great spiritual texts and teachers of the past and present tell us that compassion is the innate, natural condition of our hearts. The ultimate journey and skill of a human being is to discover how encompassing our hearts can be. Anger, hatred, and cruelty as well as kindness, forgiveness, and understanding live as possibilities within all our hearts. Our capacity to be a cause of suffering and our capacity to end suffering live side-by-side within us. The challenge and invitation of every human life is to discover the wisdom and compassion to nurture all that contributes to the end of suffering and the well-being of all who live. As much as the story of the human condition is the story of conflict and division, it is equally the story of joy and redemption. Outside the Holocaust memorial in Jerusalem, which bears witness to the murder and pain of millions, there runs a path flanked by carob trees. Beside each tree a small marker bears the name of a person who risked his or her life and safety to protect and rescue Jews. In the aftermath of the attack on the World Trade Center, thousands of unsung heroes came forth to offer food and support to the rescuers, comfort and aid to the bereaved. As Helen Keller once said, "Although the world is full of suffering; it is also full of overcoming it."

Compassion is the most precious of all gifts. In times of sorrow and bewilderment, it is what restores us and offers refuge. It is the force of empathy in your own heart that allows you to reach out and touch the broken heart of another. It is rooted in the heartfelt acknowledgement that others, like ourselves, yearn to be free from suffering and harm, and be safe and happy. It is compassion that rescues us from despair and helplessness, that provides a refuge of peace and understanding inwardly and outwardly. Compassion does not claim to be a quick fix for the age-old causes of suffering, nor is it a magic wand that will sweep away sorrow. But it is our commitment to compassion and our willingness to nurture it in every moment that gives meaning to life.

You may doubt the appropriateness of compassion, when you are faced with inexplicable acts of cruelty. At times it feels impossible to find forgiveness and understanding, when you are faced with the pain of loss, betrayal, or injustice. It is true that finding compassion is often not easy, yet the alternative is much harder. Living with anger, resentment, and alienation in your heart is more difficult. You do not need to be a saint to find the grace and transformative power of compassion; you need only be willing to pay attention to pain and its cause and to commit yourself to its end.

Listening to the Cries of the World 1

I N THE FIRST CENTURY A.D. in northern India, in what is
now possibly Afghanistan, one of the most graceful and
powerful texts in the Buddhist tradition was composed. The text
that is now known as the Lotus Sutta has as its central theme the
celebration of a powerful and boundless compassion. It describes
compassion as the expression of a liberated heart that pervades all
corners of the universe, relieving anguish, pain, and suffering
wherever it touches. It speaks about the spirit and the commitment
of the bodhisattva Avalokitesvara, the Lord of the World, dedicated
to liberating all beings from struggle and sorrow. When the Lotus
Sutta was translated into Chinese in 400 A.D., the name Kuan Yin, or
"one who hears the cries of the world," emerged, an embodiment
of compassion that continues to occupy a central place in Buddhist
teaching and practice.

Over the centuries, all the great spiritual paths have created sym-
bols, have written poems and songs, about the innate beauty of the
human heart. It doesn't matter what our spiritual, political, or
social background is, we all long for tenderness, understanding,
and safety. What gives meaning to our lives is to give and receive

the care, sensitivity, and love that nourish our spirits. When we are young and when we are old, we depend on the compassion and care of others. When we are ill, hurting, or afraid, it is compassion that restores and shelters us. When all of our certainties, defenses, and supports are stripped away, it is compassion that heals us. Compassion is the greatest of all gifts that you can offer to or receive from another. An old Zen monk once proclaimed, "O, that my priest's robes were wide enough to gather up all the suffering in this floating world."

In temples, monasteries, and homes around the world, people begin their day by reciting the bodhisattva vow:

> Though the many beings are numberless,
> I vow to save them.
> Though greed, hatred, and ignorance rise endlessly,
> I vow to end them.
> Though the path is vast and fathomless,
> I vow to understand it.
> Though enlightenment is beyond attainment,
> I vow to embody it fully.

These words may sound grandiose or idealistic. But they are simply concerned with how you choose to live your life and interact with others. What difference would it make in your life if you engaged the world with a conscious commitment to end sorrow or pain wherever you meet it? What difference would it make to wake in the morning and greet your family, the stranger beside you on the bus, the troublesome colleague, with the intention to listen to them wholeheartedly and be present for them? Compassion doesn't always call for grand or heroic gestures. It asks you to find in your heart the simple but profound willingness to be present, with a commitment to end sorrow and contribute to the well-being and ease of all beings. A word of kindness, a loving touch, a patient presence, a willingness to step beyond your fears and reactions are all gestures of compassion that can transform a moment of fear or pain. Aligning yourself with the path of understanding and compassion, you are learning to listen to the cries of the world.

The universe is full of beings, those you know and those who will forever be strangers. The world is made up of those you care for, those you are indifferent to, and those you fear or dislike. With those you love and care for, your compassion is often unhesitating; you reach out to console, support, and encourage without reservation. With those who are strangers, your response may vary. You may feel an indifference that you are ashamed of or a vague sympathy that is quickly forgotten in the busyness of your life. With those you dislike, your compassion for their suffering can be subtly mixed with an embarrassed satisfaction over their suffering. Compassion is an invitation to cross the divide that separates "us" from "them." At times these almost imperceptible barriers are lifted. You see lines of pain in the faces of refugees or the homeless woman on the street, and your heart trembles. You listen again to the anguish of the person you resent and find that your history of struggle with him is released, as the hardness of your heart begins to soften. Suddenly you are present in a new way — free of prejudice and fear. It is as if your heart has expanded, revealing all of life as one organism.

The idea that you bear the responsibility for rescuing all beings from sorrow is an impossible ideal and perhaps is even arrogant.

Compassion is a response of the present. How do you receive the person who is right before you? When you look at the myriad beings in this world, you also meet your own prejudices: There are those you are delighted to connect with and serve and those you resist, maybe thinking they deserve their pain. When you meet the hapless victim of a road accident or a child dying of cancer, your heart overflows with natural, spontaneous compassion. When you meet the person dying of cirrhosis of the liver induced by alcoholism or the person imprisoned for violence, your heart may close, and you may find yourself deaf to their cries. When you are faced with your own prejudices, you begin to understand that learning to nurture a heart without boundaries is truly a journey that asks for profound understanding, receptivity, and courage. What would your life be like if you were able to turn toward this world without discrimination or prejudice and embrace it with the care and tenderness you would naturally extend to the person you most love? Compassion invites you to receive every instance and event of sorrow as if it has etched upon it the message "understand me, hear me."

The bodhisattva vow acknowledges and accepts that greed, anger, and delusion are endless. You do not have to be perfect to be compassionate. Compassion includes the willingness to embrace in a loving and accepting way all those moments of resistance and judgment. Compassion is concerned not only with how you receive others but how you receive your own mind and heart. At times you are afraid, agitated, or cruel. These are moments of suffering. Anger, fear, and judgment are not in themselves obstacles to compassion, but they become obstacles when they are left unquestioned. In themselves, they are invitations to compassion. Can you listen to yourself in the moments when you feel most enraged, afraid, or resentful? Finding compassion for yourself in those moments is the forerunner of being able to extend compassion without conditions to others, whose rage, fear, and confusion are no different than your own. Because you can understand the pain of those experiences in your own heart and are willing to stay present and be intimate with that pain, you can find the steadfastness and courage to be present for another person entangled in the same pain.

You may be tempted to postpone compassion, feeling that you have to first complete a self-improvement project. You have to fix your anger, your selfishness, your greed, and then perhaps you can open your heart and listen to the cries of the world. But self-improvement can be an endless project; it is an expression of a judgmental belief system in which you deny compassion to yourself. You feel ashamed of your negativity, fear, and the avalanche of pettiness and criticism and believe you have to somehow erase them from your heart. Heroically, you try to banish your anger, only to find it replaced by jealousy. You may strive to overcome that and then feel proud of yourself. Pride becomes the new focus of your endeavors to perfect yourself, and then you are horrified to find it replaced by greed. At some point, it may dawn upon you that the entire project is motivated by nonacceptance and idealized notions of perfection.

A student instructed to meditate upon compassion came to his teacher in despair. "This is too hard," he complained. "I sit and try to extend compassion to the countless beings in the world, and all the time I find myself criticizing how my neighbor wears her robes, how much noise my roommate makes, how much my knees hurt, and how bad the food is. How can I ever get beyond this?" The teacher listened patiently to the long litany of complaints, then sat and pondered for a time. Hoping for words of reassurance or a shortcut to transcendence, the student waited expectantly. Finally the teacher opened her eyes and said, "These difficulties are going to be with you for the rest of your life."

Although this may not be a literal truth, it's worthwhile to question how you would respond if you knew that anger, fear, resistance, and anxiety might be lifelong companions. You could continue to deny them, condemn them, or try to purge them from your heart. Or you could explore the possibility of a radical change of heart. Is it possible to embrace all that you are most prone to condemn or fear with receptive kindness? Can you accept the moments of anger and fear as guests, be willing to receive them with kindness without feeling obliged to serve them a five-course meal? No one likes being angry or afraid, but they are not your enemies. They are painful feelings that invite investigation, understanding, and tenderness. You can learn to accept these feelings with equanimity and allow them to arise and pass without blindly identifying with them or acting upon them. It is often in the hardest moments of our lives that we find the deepest compassion. To postpone compassion is to postpone your capacity to engage with your life in the fullest and wisest way.

The bodhisattva promises that "although enlightenment is beyond attainment, I vow to embody it fully." *Embody* is a key word. Compassion is more profound than simply entertaining altruistic thoughts or idealizing some future attainment. The great teachers and mystics of the past and present have deeply inspired us because they have embodied in their words and actions the wisdom and compassion we yearn for. We admire them not just for some remarkable spiritual experience that occurred under a bodhi tree, in a desert, or on a mountaintop, but because their lives have been visible manifestations of selflessness and freedom. They inspire us not through their aloofness but through their engagement and example: the Buddha who reached out to bathe the body of a diseased monk that no one would touch, the Christ who welcomed the outcast that everyone disdained. For compassion to make a difference, it must be embodied.

We are always beginners in the art of compassion. No matter how advanced or refined we believe our understanding to be, life is sure to present us with some new experience or encounter with pain we feel unprepared for. Your partner betrays you, your teacher disappoints you, some event of unimaginable cruelty happens in the world, and once more you are asked to open your heart and receive it. "This also, this also" is the essence of compassion. Over and over you are asked to meet change, loss, injustice, and over and over you are asked to find the strength to open when you are most inclined to shut down.

Compassion is multifaceted. Over the centuries Avalokitesvara, or Kuan Yin, has been portrayed in a variety of different forms. At times she is depicted as a feminine presence, her face serene, her arms outstretched and her eyes open, embodying a warm, receptive presence. She is often portrayed seated on a lotus flower, symbolizing the opening and flowering of the heart and mind. In one hand she holds a book of teachings, symbolizing her nondualistic understanding, and in her other hand she holds a vase, signifying the pouring out of boundless love and compassion. In China, she is sometimes portrayed holding a willow branch, symbolizing her capacity to bend in the face of the most fierce storms and winds of life without being broken. The weeping willow represents her compassionate care for the pain of the world. At times Avalokitesvara is painted with a thousand arms and hands, and in the center of each hand is an eye depicting her constant awareness of anguish and her all-embracing responsiveness. Kuan Yin is also portrayed as an armed warrior, laden with a multitude of weapons. She carries a crossbow, a thunderbolt, a spear, and a shield. She embodies the fierce, uncompromising face of compassion. She is a protector and a guardian who is committed to uprooting the causes of sorrow.

Compassion is not just a feeling; it is a response to pain that is deeply rooted in wisdom. It is a commitment to alleviating suffering and the cause of suffering in all its forms. The human story is both personal and universal. Our personal experiences of pain and joy, grief and despair, may be unique to each of us in the forms they take, yet our capacity to feel grief, fear, loneliness, and rage, as well as delight, intimacy, joy, and ease, are our common bonds as human beings. They are the language of the heart that crosses the borders of "I" and "you." In the midst of despair or pain, you may be convinced that no one has ever felt this way before. Yet there is no pain you can experience that has not been experienced before by another in a different time or place. Our emotional world is universal.

Much of life is dedicated to minimizing pain and maximizing happiness. We have become more and more sophisticated in our technology — we can live in space, map the human genome, yet we have not been successful in our quest to end sorrow. Our age-old problems of prejudice, cruelty, and division persist, simply taking new forms over the centuries. For fear, separation, and sorrow to end, you must understand their cause. You can search the world for causes, but in the end you must look within yourself. Mistrust, alienation, and rage are not life sentences. They arise in your engagement with the world, and they can be transformed in your engagement with the world. The classroom of the bodhisattva is life. True compassion is not forged at a distance from pain but in its fires. Shantideva, a great Indian mystic, taught, "Whatever you are doing, ask yourself, *What is the state of my mind?* With constant mindfulness and alertness, accomplish good. This is the practice of the bodhisattva." Compassion is born of wisdom, through genuine insight into the nature of reality, through an appreciation of impermanence and all its implications, and through a willingness to be aware of suffering and its cause. Wisdom and compassion are like the two wings of a bird: Both are necessary for the bird to soar, both are necessary for our hearts to open and heal.

Compassion holds within it resilience and equanimity. Patience, receptivity, awareness, and honesty are all part of its paradigm. Forgiveness and courage and a willingness to be intimate with life give compassion its power. The willingness to surrender self-centeredness and self-righteousness form part of the character of compassion. Your willingness to explore these qualities enables you to find courage in adversity and meaning in the moments of greatest barrenness. Compassion can rescue you from despair and blame and allow you to live with dignity and integrity. Ultimately it can bring to an end the most painful separation between self and other. Compassion is sometimes defined as "the heart that trembles in response to pain" or as the capacity to "feel with." When you can truly listen to the cries of the world, you can begin to understand what Milarepa, a great Tibetan master, meant when he said, "Just as I instinctively reach out to heal and care for a wound in my leg as part of my own body, why should I not reach out instinctively to hear and care for any wound wherever it exists, as part of this body."

Suffering 2

To SPEAK ABOUT COMPASSION, we must speak about
suffering. No one likes to suffer. No one likes the
moments when our bodies are ill or in pain. No one enjoys adversity or difficult emotions. No one wants to have their heart broken
or their mind terrorized. None of us welcomes the unanticipated
events of loss, separation, and disappointment that intrude upon
the fragile calm and stability of our lives. We fear and resist the
experience of suffering; we even dislike the word. We think it is
depressing or grim to talk about suffering. We name it stress,
anguish, unease, or sorrow to make it more palatable. But the simple truth remains: We all face suffering. To have a body is to experience illness and pain and eventually death. To have a mind is to
experience confusion, turmoil, and agitation. To have a heart is to
feel hurt, loneliness, and fear. To love is to feel loss and grief.

To open to the reality of suffering is not a denial of the joy and
delight that is also part of life. It is a recognition that as long as we
deny suffering, our capacity to experience genuine intimacy and
happiness will also be limited. As difficult as it is to embrace the
simple truth of suffering, to deny it is to travel a path of much

greater hardship. To refuse to accept the suffering that will inevitably visit all of us is to accept instead a life of fear and struggle, as we strive to distance ourselves from the real and imagined pain that could happen in life. It is sometimes said that a quarter of the suffering we experience is born of uncontrollable events, and three-quarters is born of trying to avoid the first quarter. Compassion will remain a closed door as long as you close your heart to an awareness and acceptance of pain. Opening to the sorrow that exists inwardly and outwardly is simultaneously opening to the boundless compassion that can emerge from your heart.

The forms of suffering vary, but the actuality of pain affects us all. As human beings, we share the common bond both of suffering and of not wanting to suffer. There are countless threads in the fabric of suffering. You lose what you have and treasure, you don't get what you want, and you receive much that is unwelcome. Countless unanticipated events bring hurt, disappointment, and loss. Physical, psychological, and emotional pain appears in many forms. Your certainties can be shattered, your images and dreams disappointed, and there may come times when your world crumbles and you feel there is no refuge anywhere.

I lived in Asia for a number of years, and one of the most instructive experiences of that time was born of the simple reality that I rarely got what I wanted, and much of the time I got what I truly didn't want. If I wanted health, I would be struck with some exotic illness. If I wanted quiet, I got disturbance. If I wanted digestible food, I was sure to end up with the most unpalatable meal. If I wanted to find the "spiritual" Asia I had constructed in my fantasies, I would instead encounter the hustler on the street corner. Because I am a slow learner, it took some time for me to understand and accept that part of the suffering I went through was unavoidable, and that a much larger part had its roots in my aversion and resistance to what I couldn't avoid. Every day I would have endless conversations with myself about what was wrong with where I was, whose fault it was, and how it could be fixed.

Faced with a child begging on the street, I would find myself judging a society that couldn't care for its deprived people, perhaps dropping a few coins into the child's hand while making sure I kept my distance from him. I would debate with myself whether I was just perpetuating the culture of begging by responding to the child's pleas. It took a long time for me to understand that, as much as the coins may have been appreciated, they were secondary to the fact that I rarely connected with the child. Compassion is our ability to feel with. This involves a leap of imagination and a willingness to go beyond the borders of our own experience and judgments. What would it have meant to place myself within the life and heart of that begging child? What would it be like to never know if you will eat today, to have your life be dependent on the handouts of strangers? In that leap of imagination, our hearts can tremble in response to pain.

If you track a single day in your life, you will see that adversity is a daily occurrence. Your child throws a tantrum at breakfast that makes you late; the car doesn't start; it's raining and you've forgotten your umbrella; the nagging pain in your neck competes for attention with your concern about your aging parent. You pick up a newspaper to see the pictures of yet another catastrophe in the world. You are faced with heartbreak, you grieve, your health is threatened. Sometimes you feel almost overwhelmed by the pain, hunger, and terror that are the daily diet of too many people in the world.

How do you respond to all this pain, which seems bottomless and endless? There is a collective belief that suffering is bad news, a problem to solve, a mistake. You might think that pain is a punishment for something you did wrong. You might think suffering will ennoble you. Despair is a landscape we visit many times in our lives. *Why me? What did I do to deserve this?* When you are able to stop saying, *Why have these terrible things happened to me?* and can say, *Why not me?,* you have taken the first steps on the path of healing and compassion.

We will go to almost any length to try to distance ourselves from sorrow and, in truth, from life. We seek numbness in drugs, food, distraction, and addictions, as if they were the only available refuge. A fourteen-year-old boy talked about his need to take the antidepressants he had been on for a year. "It's easier," he said, "if you don't care. If you care, you get hurt. Its dangerous when you care." A study done in 1996 revealed that 600,000 children in the United States take antidepressants, and 1.5 million children in Britain have serious mental health problems, primarily depression. Suicide has become one of the most common causes of death among young men. We simply can't bear to see so much suffering. How often in moments of pain do you automatically reach out to turn on the television, open the fridge, find something to busy yourself with, or take a painkiller, mirroring the sentiments of the young boy who believes it is dangerous to feel? The alternative to these mechanisms of escape, you may believe, is to drown in the pain.

We seek control to protect ourselves from vulnerability, change, and loss. Through what we amass and possess, we endeavor to build defenses against a changing life that we perceive as hostile to our well-being. You can spend a lot of time trying to predict what might go wrong and how you can prevent it. Habits, expectations, blueprints can govern your life, all in the service of trying to make the world conform to how you believe it should be—a world without pain or disappointment. Yet none of us is invulnerable: our expectations are disappointed, our habits do not protect us from the unpredictable, and our blueprints for life constantly have to be modified. So many of our mechanisms of self-protection in themselves bring pain into our lives.

One of the primary responses to suffering is to find a way to "fix it," which is often just a way to try to get rid of it. Suffering, we believe, is unfair, and that makes us angry. Clearly anger is part of the emotional spectrum that can awaken us, spur us into wise action and intervention. It is also an emotion that is too often channeled into blame. It's like the old story of a man shot with an arrow who refuses help until he knows who fired the arrow, from which direction, and why. We console ourselves with blame; if we know whose fault it is, life feels less out of control. But if you were to reflect even for a moment upon the anger, prejudice, fear, or resentment that you experience, you would perhaps come to understand that it is impossible to trace its beginning. You might see a lineage of anger or prejudice that has run through your family for generations. What kind of hurt, what experience of pain, began that lineage? Who can you truly blame? If this is true for you, perhaps it is also true for others. You also come to understand that blame does little to bring about the end of division and sorrow; rather it is one of the ingredients of its perpetuation. What would your life be like if you stopped blaming? It might be a life in which you could attend wholeheartedly to the pain of the moment and embrace it with kindness.

Busyness becomes a defense against being still and listening to the cries of the world and the cries of your own heart. The characters in Chinese for *busyness* translate as "heart killing." You might see in your own life how busyness is an antidote for feeling deeply. A Pablo Neruda poem puts it like this:

> If we were not so single-minded
> about keeping our lives moving,
> and for once could do nothing,
> perhaps a huge silence
> might interrupt this sadness
> of never understanding ourselves
> and of threatening ourselves
> with death.
>
> Perhaps the earth can teach us
> as when everything seems dead in winter
> and late proves to be alive.
>
> Now I'll count up to twelve
> and you keep quiet and I will go.[1]

We are dedicated doers and fixers. When we encounter pain, we automatically think in terms of finding a solution. There is not always a solution to suffering, but there is always a possible response. The responses that heal lie in the compassion of your heart, in your profound commitment to being present and awake in the face of even the most dire pain. This is not a prescription for passivity. Much of the pain in this world is unnecessary, caused by greed, hatred, and prejudice. But the end of this misery will not be born of blame, anger, or fear. The choices and actions that will lead to its end must have their roots in a transformed heart. When you are willing to turn directly toward pain, receive it, and embrace it with tenderness, you have begun to embody compassion.

We have demonized pain and suffering so often that flight seems to be the only option. Rarely does anyone tell you it is a good idea to stop running and be still, that instead of fleeing from sorrow you could come closer to it, befriend it, feel and understand it. Finding the commitment to stop running from pain is the first step in cultivating compassion. Your willingness to turn toward suffering rather than away from it is the beginning of approaching the world with greater kindness and tenderness. To listen to the cries of the world, you are asked to be still, to let go of your arguments, judgments, fault-finding, and the effort to make the difficult disappear.

It is a great relief to stop running from pain. In standing still and receiving life with all its adversity and sorrow, you have withdrawn your permission for suffering to define your life. You have also withdrawn your consent to living in fear. Something profound happens in your heart when you turn with kindness toward all the circumstances of pain you have previously repressed, dismissed, or fled from. There is a softening, an opening, a deepening capacity and willingness to understand sorrow and its cause. You come to know that your willingness to be present with pain is the midwife to compassion. Turning toward sorrow in your own life opens your eyes to the immense suffering in the world. Your heart opens to all those whose lives are governed by terror, violence, hunger, and dispossession. Curiously, you do not become depressed or overwhelmed. Instead, you begin to shed some of the isolation and painful separateness born of the compulsion to defend and protect yourself. The cries of the world are also your cries. You are bonded with others in the shared yearning to be free from pain and sorrow.

Stephen Levine, author of *Who Dies?*, tells the story of an elderly woman dying with bitterness and resentment poisoning her heart. Lying in her hospital bed, she treated everyone who cared for and visited her with such contempt and anger that in time she was left alone. One night, in the midst of her pain, she said that her heart broke open, and the pain she felt was no longer just her pain but the pain of the world. The pain in her back was no different from the pain of the woman in the refugee camp, the dispossessed woman giving birth alone, the child in the cancer ward. Her rage against the injustice of her life and her illness dissolved, and she found in her heart a new power to bridge the abyss of anger that had so long divided her from others.

The Suffering Born of Loss

Suffering is born of conditions. Factors and events often outside our control combine in ways that culminate in pain. If you look carefully at many of the experiences of pain in your life, beneath the anger, resentment, and anxiety, you will find the landscape of grief. The universal and immutable law of change means that there will not only be beginnings but also endings. Beginnings signal promise, excitement, happiness, possibility. Endings signal finality, loss, and sometimes pain. We greet with delight the birth of a child, the beginning of a new project, the start of a romantic relationship, but what happens when that delightful child turns into a moody teenager who tells you she hates you, when the new project ends, when the romantic relationship turns into a war zone? You are faced with the reality of change. You are faced not only with the shifts that have taken place in your life but also with the investment you have unconsciously made in life standing still. Change is at times sorrowful, but far more painful is our refusal to accept it and align ourselves with the simple truth of impermanence and all its implications.

Change brings loss, and loss brings grief, often disguised as anger, fear, anxiety, or resentment. It seems like we suffer because of change. In truth, we suffer because of our refusal to accept life as it is. We demand reliability, continuity, and guarantees, and in so doing we invite unnecessary pain into our lives. It is as if we volunteer for suffering. With compassion, you can learn to embrace the unavoidable pain that enters your life with kindness. You can learn to find grace and balance in the endings that will always be part of life. Wisdom is constantly teaching us to let go of all that we so tenaciously cling to and identify with. You will inevitably grieve and mourn. Yet to cling to the illusion that you can make the world stand still for you is to create endless suffering. The sadness of loss opens us to appreciate in a heartfelt way the fragility of all life. The resistance, denial, and anger that can follow the unwillingness to accept loss hardens our hearts and isolates us from life and from peace.

A woman once told me of the heartache she experienced when her much-loved child died soon after birth. She said her initial numbness and grief was followed by a frenzy of rage and busyness. She demanded answers from the hospital, but they could not give any. She demanded answers from her pastor, but nothing he said could touch her broken heart. She initiated a lawsuit against the hospital, certain that the death was due to some neglect on their part. Finally, she found herself in a support group of parents who had also lost their children. Week after week, she would go and listen to one broken-hearted parent after another tell the story of their loss. No solution, advice, or prescriptions were offered. In each story, she listened to the undercurrent of pain and anguish they all shared. A profound shift began to happen, as she understood that her pain and grief were not something to fix or get rid of. The innate compassion of simply being received and listened to allowed her to listen to the cries of her own heart with compassion.

Nonattachment does not mean not caring. Compassion, wise action, and intimacy demand that you care and feel deeply. Without a profound commitment to caring, you are prone to indifference or to abandoning everyone and everything that pleads for your engagement and care. Yet subtly, that care can begin to be mixed with investment and holding, and this is when you begin to suffer in the face of change. The unrealistic demand for permanence can fix itself to anything—people, opinions, beliefs, objects, goals, even the most altruistic ideals. How do you know when attachment has replaced engagement and care? Because you become intolerant to challenge, difference, or change. You become rigid, self-righteous, defensive—and you suffer. But these experiences do not merit judgment or condemnation. They ask for compassion, for these are the places where we suffer.

When you build exalted images of others, you are disappointed when they fail to live up to your expectations. You get angry with them when they act or speak in ways that don't conform to how you need and want them to be. A student spoke of the rage and hurt she experienced when her much-loved teacher was found to have engaged in unethical behavior with some of his students. Her fury left little room in her heart for understanding or compassion. Her admiration was replaced with a demand for punishment. Her devotion was replaced with an equal degree of resentment. In all of this was an unseen and unspoken grief. There was a loss of faith and trust and a loss of the personal security that had been built upon the image of the teacher's infallibility and perfection. We can want too much from others — more than they can humanly provide. Our blame is often telling us where we need to reach more deeply for the compassion that can forgive.

The fear of disappointment can lead you to close your heart, to mistrust others, and to isolate yourself. Then life is filled with fear and loneliness. Heartache is part of the fabric of caring and intimacy. You can learn to wisely attend to the places where you are prone to idealize others and then demand perfection. You can accept our shared fallibility and accept that disappointment is the price you pay — not for caring but for investing too heavily in ideals and standards. Generosity is part of compassion. Most of us need to learn to be more generous with ourselves and with others.

It is not only the failures and imperfections of others that lead to grief and anger; your own losses also lead to suffering. Health turns to illness, youth turns to age, vigor begins to fade. You want to live with kindness and integrity, and you find it difficult to forgive yourself when you appear to fail. You have so many expectations of how you "should" be, and when you fall short of your exalted standards you suffer the same blame and condemnation you inflict upon others. You strive to be better, to be beyond blame, and in the relentless pursuit of your ideals you cease listening to the pain that is born of those impossible demands. You may think that pain is your fault, signalling some error you have made. Lost in judging yourself, you lack the calm and openness needed to respond wisely to your pain.

It is often hard to accept yourself, accept others as they are, and accept life as it is. Yet the alternative to acceptance is the darkness and struggle of resistance and separation. One of my early teachers used to endlessly admonish me to "swallow the blame." Whatever you cannot accept, you will flee from, yet it always follows you. Whatever you push away is going to bounce back at you; it is nature's law. Whatever you run from becomes your shadow. When you stop running, pushing, and resisting, you can begin to open and to understand. You stop layering suffering upon pain. When you strip away your fears and demands, you discover that there is little in this life that has to be an enemy. The illness in your body, the confusion in your mind, your most fierce opponent, the events you feel most threatened by — all ask for gentleness of heart, kindness, and compassion.

The Suffering of Wanting

Wanting is often rooted in a deeply held belief that you are not whole. You prowl the world looking for everything you believe will make you happier, more complete, more content. But when wholeness and happiness are externalized, disappointment follows. Nothing in the world can provide what you cannot give yourself. You abandon yourself, believing that if you had just a little more fame, love, security, recognition, or approval, you would finally be complete. Yet you never seem to get enough, so your quest goes on.

How often we find ourselves wanting what we don't have — the ideal relationship, a different body, a more cooperative mind, the happiness others seem to possess. But as long as you are tied to this bottomless wanting, you make yourself hostage to the unrealized. You need only take a moment to explore the quality of your heart and mind when you are entangled in wanting what you don't have to appreciate its painfulness. Your heart and mind contract, focused on the object of your desire with unwavering dedication and commitment. You feel that the pain is worth it, or that your drive is in the service of a greater happiness that is sure to arrive if you sustain and succeed in your search. At times, you are successful and have moments, perhaps even weeks or months, of satisfaction. And then the force of wanting reappears. You've lost interest in what you got, or it no longer provides the satisfaction it once did. So you set forth in pursuit of yet another possession or achievement. The cycle can go on relentlessly.

In moments of clarity, you can see the pain of being caught in this web of unfulfillment. It is exhausting and disempowering. Experience has proven that wanting causes suffering, yet oddly you try to use more wanting to get rid of suffering. You don't like what you have, where you are, or how you are, then find yourself reaching out for something else as a means of getting rid of what you are experiencing. You bounce between aversion and craving, creating such a cascade of busyness that you are deafened to the cries of your own heart. Learning to make peace with what is, to love what you have, to care for where you are, is the timeless message of all spiritual paths. It is not a surrender of vision or aspiration; it is a surrender of alienation and disconnection. To discover the end of suffering, inwardly and outwardly, you must understand the causes of suffering. How much pain in the world is born of wanting and self-cherishing? How much happiness in the world is born of acceptance, generosity, and compassion?

The Pain of Isolation

Isolation is believing that you are a separate being, living in a world of many other separate beings. You are lonely, so you reach out for comfort and companionship; you are afraid so you withdraw in fear of pain. you are endlessly preoccupied with "my" plans, "my" hopes, "my" dreams, "my" fears. You long for intimacy, connectedness, and warmth, but the barrier between you and others feels impenetrable. You are afraid of the vulnerability that may follow the letting down of those barriers, so you timidly peer over the parapets of your defenses to make contact with another. Often, at the first real or imagined sign of challenge or hurt, you withdraw. Your fear of intimacy often outweighs your longing for it, and your isolation becomes solidified.

Recently, during one of the outbreaks of violence in Northern Ireland, a journalist traced the riot back to its beginnings. A young Catholic woman and a young Protestant woman were returning to their homes with their shopping from opposite directions. They met on the pavement, recognized each other, and both refused to step aside to allow the other to pass. Insults and harsh words were exchanged with increasing intensity. A crowd began to gather and joined in the confrontation. Stones were thrown, and the impasse degenerated into a riot involving not just the two women but the whole community. People were injured, homes were firebombed, and ambulances were attacked.

Your sense of who you are is composed of everything you identify with: your race, religion, beliefs, opinions, emotions, body, and mind. None of these actually sets you apart from others, but your identification and grasping separates you. Those with whom you share common bonds of clinging become your allies. Your allies support your opinions, beliefs, and values. Those who differ become your enemies. Suffering is perpetuated through clinging, individually and collectively. The gap between self and other is not neutral. It is filled with hatred, prejudice, fear, and intolerance. If you carefully explore your sense of self and separation, you begin to realize it is an illusion perpetuated by fear.

If you were invited to write a short autobiography, beginning each sentence with "I," you would soon understand that "I" never stands alone. It is always "I am, I want, I have, I feel." Your sense of who you are continually undergoes subtle and major changes, depending on the conditions and changes in your life and in yourself. Who were you before the feeling of resentment arose or before the judgmental thought appeared? Your sense of yourself in that moment was radically different than in this one. Your isolation and sense of inhabiting an independent self is an illusion. Your sense of self is interdependent and interconnected with all selves. Your well-being, safety, and happiness is intrinsically interwoven with the well-being, safety, and happiness of all life. To rescue yourself from suffering, you are asked to commit to rescuing all beings from suffering.

Two women in nearby towns in northern Canada were forced to venture out in a fierce winter storm to attend to family emergencies. One was needed to take her pregnant daughter to the hospital, the other was called to take care of her ill father. They made their way along the road from opposite directions, through hurricane winds and drifting snow. Then they both found themselves stopped on opposite sides of a fallen tree blocking the road. It took only a few minutes for them to tell each other their stories, exchange car keys, get in the other's car, turn them around, and set forth to complete their journeys.

When I was a teenager growing up in Canada, our town bordered a Native American reservation. Although physically only an iron bridge separated the town and the reserve, emotionally and psychologically they were separated by an abyss of prejudice, mistrust, and resentment. In all my teenage years, I only spoke with someone from the reserve village a few times. On many occasions, though, I was judgmental of those I did not know.

Crossing the abyss between self and other does not always require heroic actions or gestures. It requires you to listen to the sounds of pain, to respond with compassion, and in so doing participate in the healing of pain. Isolation and division are not life sentences. You can withdraw your consent from the tactics of blame and fear that perpetuate division. You can learn to be mindful of your assumptions and labels. When you hear thoughts forming in your mind that begin with the words *You are* . . ., followed by a conclusion or definition that freezes another person into an image, you can dive beneath your concepts and question what you fear or are holding on to. You can turn those same words around and ask, *Are you . . .?* and release some of the separation. To grasp and hold to "me" and "mine" is to be lost in the suffering of separation. To release the grasping is to open the door to our intrinsic connectedness. Though there is much that is different between yourself and others, our common bond lies in our wish to be free from pain and sorrow, to be safe, happy, and cared for. Milarepa, a great Tibetan sage, once said, "Long accustomed to contemplating compassion, I have forgotten all difference between myself and others."

The Sorrow of Awareness

It can seem as if awareness makes you suffer. Awareness brings with it an increasing sensitivity and intimacy with your inner and outer worlds. You feel more deeply, are more attuned to the emotions and reactions in your heart. Awareness teaches you to read between the lines. You see the loneliness, need, and fear in others that was previously invisible. You sense beneath the words of anger, blame, or anxiety the fragility of another person's heart. Awareness opens your eyes and heart to a world of pain and distress that previously only glanced off the surface of your consciousness, like a stone skipping across the water. As awareness deepens, you find yourself listening more acutely to the cries of the world, and each of those cries has written upon it the plea to be received and understood. You feel your heart tremble in response, and it is often deeply disturbing.

A man once came on a meditation retreat to find refuge from the chaos and conflict of his life. After a few days, his face and body began to relax, and he reported that the turmoil of his mind had begun to calm. He felt he was getting what he needed from his meditation. On the fourth day, it all changed. He talked about the surges of hurt, regret, and loneliness that were shattering him. He was sure he was doing something wrong in his meditation. The peace was gone, and he begged for some strategy to rescue him from the anguish. He had pursued all the avenues of distraction that had previously served to numb him to pain: He blamed the teachers, his life, his family, and himself, yet nothing worked, and he continued to be faced with the pain in his heart. Finally, with nowhere to hide and no way to distance himself from the turmoil, he said he understood that he was feeling the pain of waking up to himself and his life. It was a pivotal moment, as he also understood that the only valid response was kindness. He turned toward the pain in his heart, as if he was holding a brokenhearted child. It was the beginning of acceptance and compassion.

We are afraid of intimacy with pain because we are afraid of helplessness. We fear that we don't have the capacity to embrace suffering, and that we have insufficient inner resources to be present with pain without being overwhelmed. Yet the more you find the willingness to embrace adversity and affliction rather than resisting it, the more you discover you are not helpless. You find within yourself levels of resilience, kindness, and balance that are the source of wise action and speech. Just as it is awareness that opens your eyes and heart to the bottomless pain in the world, it is awareness that rescues you from helplessness. Nothing can be understood or transformed without awareness. The alchemy of awareness turns despair into possibility, turns fear into strength, turns resistance into openness. Awareness is not complex or elusive. It is born in any moment you are willing to stand still, turn toward what you want to flee from, and listen wholeheartedly.

We tend to be selective in our awareness. We are willing and delighted to be aware of everything that is pleasant. We are often far less willing to open to the difficult or unpleasant. We expend a lot of effort and energy building walls to keep the disturbing at bay. We pretend that if we keep refusing to acknowledge the difficulty that lives on the other side of the walls, it will give up and go away. It doesn't work. Resistance is truly painful, and it keeps you locked in an isolated self-preoccupation that is haunted by anxiety and pain. Opening to difficulty doesn't mean being overwhelmed or out of control. The prerequisite to ending suffering is to understand it. It's easy to hate what you don't understand. It's difficult to despise anything you understand.

Joseph, an Israeli American man, recently spent several months in Israel and the West Bank with a group of eight children. Four children were Palestinian, and four were the children of Israeli settlers. The two groups lived radically different lives, yet they both lived with fear and mistrust. Initially, Joseph spent time with the groups separately, living, talking, and making friends with them. Each group of children spoke of the "others," of their feelings of being threatened, and of their experiences of violence and rage. The word *hate* came easily to them. These eight-year-old children were well-versed in the stereotypes that had divided their cultures for generations. Eventually, Joseph arranged for the children to spend a day together. He brought the Israeli children through the checkpoint into the West Bank. Their initial steps toward one another were hesitant, hampered by a lifelong inheritance of prejudice and suspicion. Then they began to find a common language in games, and they ate and laughed together. Eventually, they began to talk of their hopes, fears, and dreams. That one day was followed by several more, and as they began to trust one another, they shared not only laughter but also tears.

Nurturing compassion is not a magical formula that dispels all our fears, prejudices, and rage in some miraculous erasure. The impulses of reaction and resistance emerge so quickly and powerfully that we are hardly able to acknowledge them. We find ourselves judging, shouting, and blaming impulsively and at times habitually. But you can learn to be kind with yourself. The impulses of anger, fear, or blame do not disqualify you from compassion. You can choose how you engage and interact with the world; awareness offers you that choice. Compassion is choosing to make your home in forgiveness, understanding, and kindness, rather than in the historical reactions, divisions, and prejudices that only bring pain and separation. As you learn to be more present in your life and open your heart to the suffering you encounter, compassion begins to flower. There may still be much in the world and in your own mind that is not as you would wish it to be. but these are things you learn to make peace with.

We all experience moments of natural, unhesitating compassion that expresses itself in kindness, sensitivity, and skillfulness. These moments sometimes take you by surprise, as you discover depths of empathy and tenderness within yourself. They don't seem to be the result of any particular effort you have made or strategy you have applied. And those precious moments of intimacy often disappear as quickly as they appeared, leaving you longing to rediscover that profound openness. But compassion does not have to be an accident. You can cultivate all its dimensions — forgiveness, equanimity, resilience, commitment, kindness, and empathy. None of us lacks for opportunities that ask for the wisdom and tenderness of compassion above all else.

Compassion
for the Blameless 3

S OME YEARS AGO, I visited a children's home run by
the Sisters of Charity in Calcutta, India. When one of
the nuns took me into the children's nursery, I was stunned by the
enormity of the suffering there. Long rows of tiny babies, tightly
swaddled in blankets, nestled beside each other. In other rooms,
older children lay on seemingly endless rows of cots. Some
clutched the railings of their beds, silently crying, some mutely
rocked their bodies in some terrible rhythm of pain, while others
reached out their arms, begging to be picked up. The nuns moved
through the rooms, feeding, bathing, and speaking to the children,
yet it was clear that the nurseries held a depth of need that was
almost unanswerable. Each morning before daybreak, the nuns
would go out in vans, collecting yet more babies and infants from
the streets where they had been abandoned. In the poverty of Calcutta, it was a project without end, yet the nuns showed no signs
of distress at the magnitude of their task. Their gentleness, perseverance, and patience seemed as bottomless as the pain they were
meeting.

As our eyes open to the vast fabric of pain, with its countless threads, our hearts can quiver with both compassion and despair. Each thread tells the story of a person, like us, who longs for happiness yet is sometimes asked to bear the unbearable. For many, the terror, deprivation, and hurt they carry are born of conditions and events outside their control and choice. Streams of refugees flee from wars they don't understand. Thousands of children are orphaned as their parents die of AIDS; their gaunt, tear-streaked faces reflect their bewilderment. Drought and famine leave numberless people scavenging for the grass and leaves that may let them live one more day. An old woman is abused by unscrupulous caretakers, a teenager is raped, a child is struck with cancer. We call them victims, survivors, the unlucky. We struggle to find words to capture the magnitude of their suffering. None of these people are conscious participants in the web of suffering they are asked to bear. None of them had the power to prevent the tragedies that struck their lives. You do not have the power to undo the events and conditions that have created their pain, but you do have the power to embrace the blameless. The compassion you are asked to discover in your heart must be as bottomless as the suffering that exists.

When I was a teenager, a close friend committed suicide. Her life wasn't terrible; her family loved her, she had many friends, and she did well in school, but she was deeply unhappy. No one was very surprised when she killed herself. There was no obvious explanation for her deep unhappiness, yet it was her companion every day. Despite her efforts to enjoy things and engage with people, she felt, she said, that "life is something I only look at through a pane of glass that keeps me apart." Another friend, cycling home from work one night, was hit by a drunk driver. His head injuries and the amnesia that followed wreaked havoc with his life. He lost his job, his home, and everything he had previously relied on. Nothing he could have done would have prevented the tragedy from scarring his life. The son of a friend, an aspiring and successful athlete, went in days from having a cold to suffering an almost total collapse of his immune system that left him on life support, fighting to survive. All of our lives have been touched by similar stories of pain. No one can create defenses strong enough to keep the unpredictability of life at bay.

In your own life too, unanticipated events and uninvited pain have visited, crumbling your certainties and leaving you bereft. You can be dedicated to wise choices, yet nothing can protect you from unexpected experiences that can break your heart. Despite efforts to cultivate honesty, integrity, and clarity, you still can find yourself the recipient of another's rage, ignorance, or prejudice. These are the moments when you are asked to dive deeply within to find the stillness and healing that rescues you from drowning in reciprocal anger or despair.

Despair is one of the near enemies of compassion. When you feel helpless to relieve or change the pain you meet, your helplessness can lead to panic, panic to despair. When you surrender to despair, something dies in your heart. You want to withdraw from life, close your eyes and your heart. Numbness may feel more attractive and safe than the vulnerability of awareness. You resign yourself to the impossibility of finding an end to suffering, and you think, *Why bother? What difference does my commitment or compassion make?* Indifference becomes a cloak to protect yourself from despair. But the price of indifference is the pain of separation and disconnection from all of life.

At times, when faced with suffering that feels too much bear, it is compassionate to give yourself the permission to back off a little. A woman told me of her escalating levels of distress as she tried to meet the needs of her young family and her aging, frail parents. In the midst of this vortex of need, she was diagnosed with breast cancer. Even in the midst of her own grief and illness, she continued her relentless endeavors to ensure that everyone in her life was safe and happy. She believed, she said, that it would be an unbearable failure to step back from caring for those around her. Guilt and obligation governed her days, until she collapsed from exhaustion. It required an enormous shift in understanding for her to see that to care for others while neglecting herself is not compassion. Taking time to listen to the signals of her body and heart meant sacrificing the role of being the perfect "carer."

Knowing when to step back in the face of pain is not a denial of suffering but an offering to yourself of the breathing space needed to garner your inner resources of balance and calm. You are recognizing that the clarity needed to respond in an effective way is momentarily lost. A compassionate and wise response is not born in the ground of panic. Learning to care for and listen to others cannot be separated from your ability to care for and listen to yourself. The inner confidence you need to embody compassion in the face of sorrow is undermined when you feel swamped or overwhelmed by pain. That confidence is deepened when you can meet the terrible, the painful, with a calm resolve to stay connected and present.

Despair is born of insisting that life be something other than it is. Despair can be the price you pay for demanding that your expectations be met and that your actions produce a visible result. You reach out to a person in pain with words of comfort and a genuine willingness to be present with them. Then you become impatient, wanting the person's pain to end so you can feel better. The point when compassion becomes interwoven with expectation or demand can be extraordinarily subtle.

There is much to learn from despair, if you listen to it whole-heartedly. Why do you become disheartened? Are you subtly try-ing to control the uncontrollable and panicking as you realize it may not be possible to do so? Do you hold within yourself, even as you reach out to touch the pain of another, a subtle timetable and agenda of change, which is then disappointed? Profound com-passion invites an equally profound willingness to let go of all your expectations, demands, and insistence. Learning to meet suffering with an open and compassionate heart is deeply humbling. All your strategies, formulas, and prescriptions are rendered ineffective by the intensity of pain you encounter. All that is left is your capacity to remain steadfastly present and engaged. Often, that is all that is needed.

A woman once told me of the nightmare she endured when her son descended into heroin addiction. In some way, he became a stranger, stealing from her and abusing her when she refused to give him the money he needed to support his habit. He would dis-appear for days or weeks, yet he would always return, needing her. He would come back filled with remorse and apologies, resolving to kick his habit. Yet within days, he would once more succumb to his addiction. She spoke of the fine line she walked between her desperate need to save her son and her unwillingness to partici-pate in feeding his addiction. All that was left to her was to love him, to hold him when he wept, to listen to him, and to be steadfast in her willingness to be present for him. "I could not give up the habit for him," she said. "I could not stop him from killing himself with the drugs, I couldn't make him want to give up his craving for the very thing that was destroying him—all I could do was help him to remember how loved and valued he was."

Compassion asks you to accept that it is impossible to end all the suffering in the world, yet you must respond as if it were possible. You embrace the impossible, yet live as if all things were possible. This is the great paradox of the compassionate heart. You enter into all moments and meet all suffering with the heartfelt wish that it would end, even as you accept that it may not be possible for you to end it. You honor the aspiration that seeks the end of all sorrow. That aspiration, when released from expectation and demand, matures into a compassion that knows no boundaries. When you find yourself frustrated and impatient with situations that don't change according to your wishes, you are in truth frustrated with your own inability to govern the ungovernable. You want people to be happy and free from suffering, but the wisdom of compassion asks you to acknowledge your own boundaries and the limits of your power. You cannot make someone happy; you cannot make suffering go away. You can only be present, and in that engagement with life, you are never helpless.

Despair can feel like a surrender to hopelessness, yet strangely you find a transforming wisdom within hopelessness. Letting go of hope does not mean yielding to depression or paralysis. Hope is the hook that keeps you waiting for the next moment to arrive rather than embracing the moment you are in. Hope is wanting to be somewhere and be someone better than where you are and who you are. Your reaction to suffering is instinctive; you want to be rid of it, and in so doing you rob yourself of the present and your capacity to embrace it. Not long ago, the young son of a friend became ill. As I sat beside him as he cried with fever and pain, I found myself telling him, "Don't worry, this will soon get better." How often do you attempt to reassure yourself and others with similar words, leaning forward into the next moment? Words of consolation and reassurance can carry within them the unspoken belief that the restoration of your own or another's well-being depends on the demise of the difficult. Of course, you hope that things will get better, that illness will turn to health, loneliness to intimacy, and chaos to peace. But too often that hope subtly turns into an insistence that life be different than it is.

Hope charged with denial and demand opens the door to fear and disappointment, which can send you cascading into despair. Sometimes giving up hope, which may only be disguised resistance and demand, is what allows you to relax with where you are and how things are in this moment. Giving up this kind of hope is what allows you to open to the uncertainty that is intrinsic to life. The truth is, you just don't know—you don't know how events will unfold, what changes will occur, or how your life will end up. Giving up hope doesn't disable our resolve; it focuses that resolve on the moment you are in rather than a moment that doesn't exist. You cultivate compassion, loving kindness, and generosity as much as you can in every moment. You don't know what effect it will have, if any, yet that uncertainty is no obstacle. You recognize that it is the very cultivation of those qualities that gives meaning to life.

A woman told me how her membership in Amnesty International had opened her eyes to the torture and cruelty suffered by people around the world every day, as they languished, often forgotten, in prison cells and labor camps. Initially, when she zealously wrote letters to political leaders, prison governors, and guards asking for the humane treatment or release of a prisoner, she found herself waiting for replies or acknowledgement, for news that her action had made a difference. She fantasized about a prison guard undergoing a radical change of heart as he read her appeals for compassion. At times, she became discouraged and stopped writing the letters. Then she came to realize that she could never sustain a commitment that depended on being answered or recognized. She still writes letters several times a week, never knowing whether they make the slightest impact, not even knowing if anyone reads them, yet she has a deep confidence that the writing makes a difference.

A Chinese proverb says, If you keep a green bough in your heart, the singing bird will come. Compassion invites you to always keep a green bough in your heart. Meeting unbearable suffering brings great sadness, but sadness is not unbearable. Sadness is the ground in which love and compassion grow. Trusting in your own resilience and cultivating an unwavering resolve rescues you from despair. You are never crushed by sadness, but you can be crushed by the surrender to despair. You witness suffering in those you love, those you don't know, and in yourself. You grieve, weep, and long for it to end. You may feel it is too much to bear, yet it is in the midst of pain that you discover your powers of resilience. You cannot conquer sadness by destroying it; instead you can accept it as part of the tapestry of life that also holds joy, empathy, and delight. Sadness destroys you only when you attempt to do battle with it. Acceptance of sadness allows you to embrace it with compassion.

Through your willingness to meet sadness in your own heart, you can learn to find room for all the possible sadness and pain in the world. Allowing all possible sadness to enter your heart also makes room for immeasurable compassion and love.

The green bough in your heart is like the willow branch that can bend in the most fierce storms of life, yet always springs back upright. It may take some time for the branch to spring back, but you can have faith that the resilience that enables you to remain present and committed will be found. Those moments when uprightness and steadiness feel remote or impossible require great patience. You can never predict when the storm will end, but it always does. Remaining committed to ending pain allows you to embrace the pain of this moment rather than looking for the end of the storm.

Resolve

Resolve is a powerful antidote to despair. The meaning and direction that bring depth to life rest upon the values and aspirations you treasure. Resolve is what translates your aspirations into reality. Without resolve, your aspirations easily become just good ideas or dreams. Over and over, you are asked to discover what in this life is worthy of your wholehearted commitment. What your mind dwells upon and is fascinated by reveals the values you hold. You can pursue the ephemeral pleasures of fame, money, security, and recognition and see the consequences of your pursuit in disappointment, anxiety, and fear of failure. Compassion invites you to aspire to an awakened heart, to trust in its value and be committed to its realization. To hold in your heart and mind the resolve to bring an end to suffering, wherever you meet it, is a transforming motivation that shapes the way you relate to conflict and loss. It is the motivation that allows you to step out of arguing, blaming, avoiding, and the ceaseless efforts to fix the world. Resolve is not about finding an answer to suffering; it is your willingness to open and embrace pain.

Especially in moments of distress, you may find yourself making a profound commitment to awakening. It is said there are no atheists in foxholes. But once the painful event recedes, you can easily become forgetful. It's like taking a walk in the woods and becoming so fascinated with the patterns of light coming through the trees that you wander off the path and become lost. Compassion doesn't demand that you ignore the great beauty in life and fixate on suffering; it does ask that you keep your eyes on the path. Your commitment to bringing about the end of pain and suffering, wherever it arises, is not something you resolve only once in your life. It is a commitment you renew again and again; every moment of pain you meet asks for its renewal. Resolve means that you keep showing up for life, with all its pain and disappointment. You can never measure the worth of your actions, but genuine compassion does not concern itself with measuring. It is the simple reality of being willing to be present and responsive that is the visible face of your commitment to the end of pain.

Resolve is relevant not only to your relationship with the world around you but also to the rhythms of your own heart and mind. Your commitment to healing and compassion asks you to withdraw your consent from dwelling in patterns of resentment, jealousy, and demand. These patterns undermine resolve and your capacity to realize the compassion that is possible. Their perpetuation relies on the tendency to linger in them. The commitment to compassion is an inner and outer journey. You are learning to radically alter the course of your heart and mind, moment to moment. Fear, judgment, and anger still arise, but you can refrain from wallowing in them.

When you encounter people in tremendous anguish from events inflicted on them by others, it is tempting to join the chorus assigning blame and demanding retribution. It is always easier to hate and blame than to understand and embrace the difficult and painful. You can become intoxicated by anger and hatred, even as they diminish you. Anger and despair are closely related. It takes great resolve to travel a middle path between the two. Compassion doesn't make you suffer; it does make you feel deeply.

There is an ancient Chassid story in which a rabbi is asked which is the right way, that of sorrow or that of joy. He answers,

> There are two kinds of sorrow and two kinds of joy. When a person broods over the misfortunes that have come, when they cower in a corner and despair, that is a bad kind of sorrow. The Divine Presence cannot dwell in a place of dejection. The other kind of sorrow is the honest grief of a person who knows what is lacking and what is needed. The same is true of joy. One who is devoid of inner richness and in the midst of empty pleasures and who does not feel or try to fill the lack is a fool. One who is truly joyful is like someone whose house has burned down, who feels a need deep in his heart and begins to build anew. Over every stone that is laid his heart rejoices.[1]

Empathy and Pity

Pity is the poor cousin of compassion. Compassion is to feel with, pity is to feel for. There is a remoteness in pity that is alien to compassion; we feel sorry for those in pain. Pity is often interwoven with condescension: *I'm sorry you're suffering, but I'm glad it's not me.* We see an innocent person enduring violence, hunger, or terror, and we wish them to be safe and protected, we pity them, yet our hearts do not tremble. Sometimes we pity ourselves, saying, *Poor me, isn't it terrible what I am being asked to endure.* Pity is the visible face of fear and resistance. We are afraid of opening, of coming too close to suffering, for fear we will be overwhelmed or devastated. Pity maintains the distance we believe protects us and at the same time absolves us of the need to feel deeply, with its implication of being asked to engage directly.

A woman, badly burned in a fire, spent months in the hospital in agony, undergoing many skin grafts. Friends, neighbors, and relatives came to visit. Over the months, she said, she came to know the difference between pity and compassion. "People who pitied me liked to keep their distance. They also didn't like being silent. They had to tell me how sorry they were for me, how bad they felt. I started to feel bad, because they felt so bad. I could sense them struggling to find the right words of consolation. I knew they loved and cared for me, and I wished I could tell them that it was okay not to have the words. They would always have one eye on the clock. I could sense their longing for visiting hours to be over so they could leave. They didn't know how to sit still. They would squirm in the chair, rearrange the flowers and cards. They were good people, good friends — they were just so afraid of my pain.

Maybe they thought it was infectious. Others could come close and not seem to feel obliged to do anything. If I was in too much pain to be touched, they would just sit beside me. Their compassion was somehow embedded in their body language — how they sat, touched, and looked at me. That I could be seen by another who didn't flinch was what gave me the courage to look into a mirror the first time after the fire."

Pity maintains separation; compassion dissolves separation. Pity does not allow you to see yourself in another. It's not that you don't want to bridge the gap that exists between yourself and another, but you are afraid to. Compassion does not exempt you from fear, but it is fierce in its commitment not to be governed by fear. Consenting to fear is what divides and separates us. In pitying another person, you cease to respect them. You then see them as less than whole, somehow imperfect. Respect is part of authentic compassion. Suffering does not diminish a person or make them imperfect. In parts of Asia, the disabled and sick are welcomed and served with reverence; they are seen as offering the opportunity for people to develop compassion and selflessness. In Tibet, people were taught to regard the beggars and the sick as buddhas in disguise, come to encourage us to develop compassion. A Tibetan lama once asked his student to pray that, if he was reborn, it would be in a hell realm, because that is where compassion is most needed.

Compassion needs empathy, just as a boat needs water. The words "my pain," "your pain," "my grief," "your grief," "my fear," "your fear" make no sense in the domain of empathy. The compassionate heart recognizes the universality of all sorrow. All beings are bonded in their capacity to experience the whole spectrum of emotion. Our compassion too must traverse all boundaries. Empathy invites you to cross the borders of your own mind and heart, and all that you cling to, to acknowledge our interconnectedness.

Your life story is different from the life story of a woman living in a Soweto township or a child abandoned in a refugee camp. You may never know what it is like to lose your home and see your family disappear in the tides of war; you may never be dispossessed of your country and everything you love to seek asylum in a strange land. You may never know what it is like to be hated and abused because of the color of your skin, your gender, or your religion. You may never know what it is to be an abuser. There will always be realms of experience, both joyful and sorrowful, that will never be part of your life, but they are part of someone's life. Our stories differ but our hearts do not.

Compassion does not require you live someone else's story or endure their suffering. It asks you to open your heart to embrace the realities that are held within all life. We have all known what it feels like to be lonely, afraid, and bereft. In the moments of pain in your own life, what is it that heals and supports you? It is not the catalog of good advice, formulas, or opinions that may be offered. We are healed through compassion and love.

Empathy is not standing at a distance from the pain of the world. It is standing within it, learning to take your seat in the fire. Empathy is the ability to place yourself in the heart of another, to listen to the waves of pain and anguish they feel, and to feel those waves within yourself. Empathy is an art of intuition and wise imagination. It is a dissolving of the divide that seems to separate you from others. A Native American proverb says, If you want to understand a person, walk a mile in their moccasins. If you want to understand the pain of another, live a few moments in their heart.

I once read a story about a prisoner who murdered a prison guard and was given a life sentence with no human contact. For the rest of his life, he would see no one, and no one would speak to him or touch him. His cell was without windows, and all shiny surfaces were removed so he could not even see himself. Rightly, his jailers knew that this banishment from all human contact was the worst punishment that could be dispensed. If we could let go of our own judgments of right and wrong, deserved and undeserved, we could perhaps glimpse the suffering of his life.

In the Tibetan tradition of Buddhism, the meditative practice of giving and receiving is part of the training in developing a compassionate heart. The practice is to sit quietly, letting your body settle into a deep sense of ease and well-being, letting your mind relax and calm. You then imagine or visualize someone in front of you as vividly and clearly as possible, someone who is suffering. You try to sense as deeply as possible all the ranges of suffering of that person: their fear, rage, loneliness, distress, and anger. You let the ripples of their anguish flow through you. You visualize all the pain gathering together like a storm cloud that dissolves as you breathe it in. As you breathe out, you visualize that you are sending out a cooling light of peace, happiness, and well-being to the person in front of you.

The practice and cultivation of compassion is about breaking down the barriers of self. Giving and receiving can be cultivated in the face of any event or moment of suffering you meet in life. Every day gives you innumerable opportunities to open your heart to pain. You see a young child weeping inconsolably, a hunched elderly woman for whom every step is torture, the gaunt-faced teenager who asks you for money on the street. You turn on the television, and the news invites you to sense the human pain and torment behind the images and sound bites. In all these moments, you can turn away from life or turn toward it. Be careful not to let yourself be distracted in those moments or to let your compassion run aground in blame or indifference. Empathy invites you to be vulnerable, to allow the spark of compassion be ignited by all that you see. You are witnessing only a tiny fraction of the pain in the world, but it is enough to open the door of your heart so you can give and receive.

Responsibility

When I first began to practice meditation, I turned up eagerly for the first sessions with my teacher, anticipating that I would be introduced to esoteric practices and initiations. I was disappointed and somewhat insulted, particularly when my teacher told me that I was not mature enough to meditate. Instead, I was instructed for the first months to spend hours each day reflecting upon my motivation, contemplating cause and effect and interconnectedness, and nurturing compassion. Although I was reluctant to admit it, my motivation for wanting to meditate was extraordinarily self-centered. I was searching for transcendental experiences, self-improvement—basically looking for a way to maximize my own happiness and decrease my personal pain. In the eyes of my teacher, the only authentic reason to practice meditation was to bring about the end of suffering, wherever it existed, through wisdom and compassion.

One of the first instructions I was given was to reflect on appreciation and gratitude. Geshe Rapden, an esteemd Tibetan monk who was appointed by the Dalai Lama to teach Westerners, told me to imagine a blind turtle, living on the ocean floor, that rose to the surface of the sea once every hundred years. On the surface of the ocean floated a golden ring. The chances of the surfacing turtle getting its head through the ring were as rare, he said, as the opportunities and freedoms that I took for granted. The freedom we have to listen, to nurture awareness, and to explore inwardly is a tremendous privilege. We are not bound simply to ensuring our survival, satisfying our hunger, or protecting ourselves from danger. Compassion is not just a spiritual exploration; it also has political, ethical, and environmental implications. The ethical dimension of compassion would suggest that privilege carries the responsibility of bringing to fruition the safety and ease of all those who are banished to the shadows of life through poverty and oppression. Compassion invites us to participate in the healing of the world.

Healing is not just an abstract notion of doing good. In listening to the cries of the world, you hear the cry for attention, tenderness, forgiveness, tolerance, and understanding. Responsibility is your capacity to respond wholeheartedly to those cries. You do not have to look far for the opportunity. Do you take the time to listen to the pain lurking behind the words of anger that a colleague speaks to you? Do you reach out to the stranger who asks for just a moment of your attention? Do you look into the eyes of the person you are most prone to dismiss? Do you take the time to telephone the friend who you know is struggling and distressed? These are the moments when compassion moves from the abstract to genuine engagement.

The responsibility and responsiveness that is part of the fabric of compassion is radically different from the exaggerated personal responsibility that is often guilt in disguise. You are not asked to adopt grandiose ideas of saving the world, to care for others just because you are more affluent and privileged than they are. Responding to pain out of guilt rarely heals and is usually unsustainable. You can "perform" good acts, give to charity, and then feel you have paid your dues, but your heart can remain untouched. The responsibility of compassion comes from recognizing that you have the freedom to give, and offering your attention and tenderness becomes as instinctive as caring for your most beloved child. You may not be able to save the world, but you can touch the person in front of you with all the compassion and care that you can embody.

By nurturing compassion, you also take responsibility for your own heart and mind. Each one of your actions leaves an impression on the hearts of others. The clarity or confusion, the love or resentment you cultivate inwardly makes its mark upon the world. Every single thing you think, speak, or do has consequences and creates ripples of effect. Understanding this more and more deeply, you learn to take care with your thoughts and actions. They can be guided by wisdom and compassion or by fear and anger.

A much-loved teacher once remarked, "If you plant an apple seed, you are not going to grow a mango tree." In every moment of life you are planting seeds that will come to fruition. Responsibility asks you to be ever aware of what kind of seeds you are planting. Shantideva, the great Indian teacher and poet who wrote extensively on compassion, said, "A person who is traveling the path of compassion will always be aware, What is the state of my mind? With constant mindfulness and alertness accomplish good;

this is the practice of the compassionate ones." It is unlikely that healing and tenderness will spring from states of agitation, anger, or fear. The responses of compassion that truly make a difference in the life of another are born of clarity and sensitivity. The responsibility that comes with the freedoms you have is the responsibility to attend to where your mind dwells and what you cultivate in your own heart.

After his enlightenment, the Buddha got up from his seat beneath the bodhi tree and opened his heart to the countless beings in the world who want happiness and find suffering. He saw the potential for freedom in others and his responsibility to nurture that potential. He renounced transcendence and engaged with the world, dedicating his life to teaching the path to the end of suffering. He summarized his path with the simple words, "I teach only one thing — that there is suffering and there is the end of suffering."

GUIDED MEDITATION
Compassion for the Blameless

The first person that you focus upon in compassion practice is someone who is in the midst of great physical, psychological, or emotional suffering. It should not be a person you are deeply attached to or intimate with. Begin by finding two or three phrases that give language to the intention you hold for that person. Select phrases that are succinct and simple. It is important that the words you use are meaningful to you. You may need to experiment to find the phrases that articulate your most genuine wish. Once you find the phrases that are meaningful, stay steady with them rather than continually altering them.

Find a space and time in which you can sit quietly and relax, removed from distractions. Let your eyes close, and invite into your attention and heart someone who is in the midst of great hardship or pain. If possible, visualize that person, their face or their circumstances. Imagine them in front of you, as vividly as possible, and try to sense every aspect of that person's distress or anguish. Sense how your heart may begin to open to their reality, with all its tragedy and struggle. Consciously bring into that reality your heartfelt wish for the relief of their suffering and for their well-being. At a pace that feels comfortable, begin to use the phrases of compassion, sustaining as fully as possible the connection you feel with that person in distress:

> May you be free from fear and danger.
> May you be free from sorrow and pain.
> May you find peace.

You may wish to use phrases that are more directly attuned to the circumstances of that person's turmoil. It might be that freedom from the pain they are experiencing is not possible, so more appropriate phrases might be:

> May you find healing.
> May you find peace in this sorrow.
> May you find ease in your heart.

As you say the phrases silently, let them rest and resound in your being. Let your intention fill your whole body and mind, let your heart soften and open. As much as possible, sustain your attention to both the phrases and the person you have invited into your heart. There will be moments when other thoughts intrude, your mind wanders, or you lose the sense of meaning behind the words. In those moments, just return to the present, renewing your connection with the person in distress. At times, you might sense that the compassion you feel begins to turn to despair, resistance, or fear. This is not a mistake; it is not something to struggle with or judge. You can let the phrases drop for a time, and anchor yourself in your breathing, body, or listening for a few moments. Renew your sense of balance and attention, and then return to the practice.

> May you be free from fear and danger.
> May you be free from sorrow and pain.
> May you find peace.

Initially, it is often helpful to cultivate this practice in some seclusion and silence. As the phrases and the intentions begin to feel more natural and spontaneous, you will discover that the practice of compassion is one you can cultivate in all the moments and circumstances in which you encounter distress and sorrow. Walking down the street, sitting on the train, listening to the heartache of another — you can meet those moments with an open and tender heart. You learn that you can open without losing your sense of balance or being overwhelmed. Each day will beckon you to attend in a compassionate way countless times, and you find that it is possible to do so.

Compassion for Those Who Cause Suffering 4

W HEN I FIRST ENCOUNTERED the Tibetan community in exile in India, I anticipated meeting a people
crushed and broken by tragedy. They had endured unimaginable
loss and pain — their families had been killed or imprisoned, many
had been tortured and uprooted from their homes, and each of
them had undertaken the long trek over the Himalayas, hunted,
frozen, and starving, to find safety in India. I was stunned to meet
a people whose hearts were amazingly intact. They grieved, cried,
and expressed anger, yet bitterness and the desire for vengeance
were markedly absent from their emotional landscape. Compassion and faith were evident everywhere. So too was the unshakable
resolve to find freedom — not only the freedom of their homeland
but, more significantly, freedom within their own hearts.

The classroom of compassion is situated in the midst of the
deepest pain and suffering. Faced with the suffering of those you
love, compassion and empathy arise naturally. Faced with people
who inflict pain, you need to dive deeply within yourself to listen
and understand. Compassion asks you to make the radical leap in
your own consciousness to embrace the perpetrators of harm. It is

hard practice, but genuine compassion embraces all suffering—the anguish of the blameless and the anguish born of hatred, ignorance, and fear. The mountain of suffering in the world can never be lessened by adding yet more bitterness and hatred to it. The spirals of fear and division are perpetuated by every gesture of rage and retaliation. You swallow the terror and rage, and you become it. Thich Nhat Hanh, a great Vietnamese Buddhist teacher and author of *Being Peace*, said: "Anger and hatred are the materials from which hell is made." To discover a heart without boundaries, you must discover compassion without boundaries.

Just as suffering can be the forerunner of bitterness and despair, it can equally be the forerunner of a deeper wakefulness and the first steps on a path of healing. You can flee from pain, ignore it, or place blame, or you can find the courage to turn toward it. The sorrow you believed yourself unable to endure can, in being embraced, become a profound turning point in your life. In the darkest moments, you can find a strengthening of your commitment to understand what compassion is. Facing the immensity of the suffering in the world, you come to see the pathways that are open to you. You can align yourself with hatred, bitterness, and division, joining the perpetrators of pain in their nightmare. Or you can learn to open, to commit yourself to healing. In the quiet whispers of your heart, you intuitively know the pathway you are called upon to travel.

At every turn, you face events and situations that test the limits of your compassion, tolerance, and understanding. There are tragedies in the world that break your heart, acts of violence and oppression that feel too much to bear and impossible to comprehend. You may find yourself adrift, wondering how you could possibly understand the heart of someone who inflicts pain upon the innocent. The possibilities of terror and danger live on the periphery of your consciousness. Your mechanisms of self-protection are endlessly provoked to the surface. In the face of threat, you find yourself striking out. Resistance and rage are assumed to be instinctive reactions to pain, but in truth they are impulses governed by fear. You contract, tempted to abandon the trembling of your heart. Separation and distance appear to promise safety, and you are tempted to build ever-higher walls to hide behind. Even numbness can seem attractive, offering a temporary sanctuary. Yet the attraction to numbness coexists with your deepest yearnings for intimacy and unity. You discover that there is no true safety behind the barriers you build; the terror and mistrust born of isolation flourish in that ground. The monster in the dark grows bigger and more solid in your refusal to meet it.

You can only hate from a distance; you can only love and understand through closeness. To find compassion in the midst of pain, you need to have a relationship to the pain. Vietnam veterans, like soldiers in wars through all of time, speak of the distance and disengagement they cultivated to enable them to fight. The psychology of hatred relies upon making your enemies less than human so you can find the permission and will to harm them. You do not always see the ways in which you make yourself less than human in the process, the damage you wreak upon your own heart. The psychology of compassion relies upon you seeing what is human —seeing yourself—in all your enemies. The person you hate or feel the most bitter toward is, in the beginning and the end, someone who wakes in the morning wanting to be safe and free from pain, someone who is healed by a loving touch, who longs for tenderness and understanding. Only when you see yourself reflected in the eyes and heart of another can you understand that to harm another is to harm yourself. As Gandhi once said, "Where there is hate and fear, we lose the way of our spirit."

Compassion asks you to cross the borders that have been constructed in your own heart through fear, prejudice, and mistrust. You must ask yourself where you wish to make your home — in the endlessly fearful and fraught country of isolation and terror or in the country of understanding and compassion. A woman once told me of the years she spent hating a person who had abused her. Long after her abuser had physically departed from her life, he continued to govern her heart. In a very real way, he had dominion over her happiness and well-being. Bitterness and resentment filled her days, poisoning her relationships. Exhausted from the ongoing struggle, she spoke of the moment when she understood that the only way she could find an end to the suffering was to be intimate with it. To live a life pervaded by bitterness and hatred is like being locked in a burning house — and then to remember that you hold the key to the door in your own hand.

You should not be ashamed of anger; compassion is not a surrender of discriminating wisdom. Compassion has a ferocity born of the capacity to unflinchingly identify the causes of sorrow and pain. Compassion is vaster than a feeling; it finds its expression in wise action. The courage, balance, and resolve needed to end suffering are made manifest through the words and acts that are bridges to the world around you. A person without anger is probably a person who has not been deeply touched by the acts of violence, oppression, and prejudice that scar the lives of too many individuals and communities. The vast amount of suffering in the world is unnecessary. It is not intrinsic to life but intrinsic to fear, blindness, and hatred.

Anger awakens you; it can be a catalyst for furthering pain or for ending it. It can degenerate into bitterness and resentment, or it can be translated into the understanding and action that heal suffering. Your dedication to compassion is tested in the fires of anger. Anger can be the beginning of abandonment or the beginning of connection; this is the choice you are asked to make again and again in life. It is not difficult to see that the most cruel and violent people in this world are those who are most disconnected from others and most disassociated from their own hearts. The most compassionate people are not those who are immune to suffering but those who have refused to follow the pathways of disconnection. Genuine compassion begins the moment you withdraw your consent from abandonment. It doesn't mean that anger will suddenly stop, but anger will no longer end your connection with other people. A compassionate heart will feel anger and fear; wisdom teaches that you do not need to perpetuate them.

A much-revered teacher was once asked if he ever felt angry or anxious and, if so, how he dealt with these emotions. He seemed surprised at the question and answered that of course he had moments of fear and anger. When he could find no other way of embracing them, he would go for advice to his own teachers, one of whom happened to be 850 years old. You can find within yourself a depth of commitment and wisdom that calls you again and again to understand what is true and liberating, what heals suffering and brings it to an end, even in the midst of the most fraught moments of life.

Rage and bitterness shatter us; they destroy the equilibrium of our own hearts and lives. This is a simple truth. Shantideva, a great Indian mystic, taught that the mind cannot find peace, nor appreciate delight or joy, nor find rest or courage, as long as the thorn of hatred dwells in the heart. There is nothing that can make an angry person happy. Unruly beings are like space; there is not enough time to overcome them all. Yet if we are able to uproot our thoughts, it is like defeating all of our enemies. You can be crushed by anger or awakened by it. To find a pathway through anger, you are asked to take the first step of releasing blame. Blame binds you to the unending song of resentment; it can paralyze you. You replay the story in an endless loop, blaming those who misuse power, those who abuse the vulnerable. The continued retelling of the story can become a substitute for action.

It is hard to release blame, but it may be the only thing that allows you to move beyond despair. You may also begin to understand that, as hard as it is to release blame, it is a much greater hardship to hold on to it. You are locked into an unwelcome marriage with those you hate and condemn; you become a cause of your own suffering. Your life comes to resemble the lives of the Japanese soldiers found on a Pacific Island in the 1950s, still fighting a war that had ended long before. Tragedy, misfortune, and all the blame and mistrust born of them become the reference point in a life you cannot fully live.

In 1996, when the Truth and Reconciliation Council met in post-apartheid South Africa, the releasing of blame that took place was the beginning of healing. The council was born of the realization that it would be impossible to punish every act of violence and harm that had occurred during the decades of apartheid. There were not enough prisons to hold all the perpetrators of violence.

In the council sessions, torturers faced the people they had tortured, jailers faced the people they had beaten and imprisoned, killers faced the grieving families of those they had killed. The perpetrators took upon themselves the commitment to listen — and thus to overturn a legacy of division, mistrust, and hatred that had haunted their lives. Each person was given the space to be heard, to speak the truth of their pain and heartache, fears and hopes. Oceans of tears were shed in that room; there was no magic wand to erase the terrible acts that had happened. But in the listening, a possibility arose, a beginning of laying down the burden of pain, a possibility of a change of heart. Archbishop Desmond Tutu spoke of the alchemy of the council, saying, "When we had listened to the testimony of people who had suffered grievously, and it all worked itself out to the point where they were ready to forgive and embrace the perpetrators, I would frequently say, I think we ought to keep quiet now. We are in the presence of something holy. We ought metaphorically take off our shoes because we are standing on holy ground."

We are prone to idealize those who find nobility of heart in the midst of the greatest suffering. In reality, they are ordinary people, like any of us. To call them survivors would be to diminish their courage and commitment to healing. They have not transcended sorrow; their hearts still ache and grieve. Sometimes, in the midst of the greatest bitterness and resentment, you come to realize that you can never heal your own spirit as long as bitterness lives there. To rescue yourself, you must rescue those who have harmed you from the power of your own rage.

Releasing the burden of blame and hatred can, at times, only happen in the aloneness of your own heart. The people who have harmed you personally through their words or acts may feel no remorse, nor any willingness to listen to the consequences of their violence. The people you will never meet who have taken part in inflicting pain and terror may continue to uphold the righteousness of their acts. It is easier to forgive someone who truly wants to be forgiven. The challenge of compassion is to make no distinctions. Compassion asks you to see beneath events, to understand that acts of terror and harm are born of suffering and lead to suffering. Suffering is not just pain; it is also blindness and self-righteousness. If your anger is directed anywhere, it should be toward hatred, fear, and ignorance. If your commitment to compassion is to make a difference, it must be a commitment to ending the causes of suffering. Shantideva taught that if you become angry with those who harm you by their words or acts, you need to understand that the inflictor of pain is also harmed by their hatred and anger. Rather than being enraged with the wielder of the stick, you should be angry with the hatred.

Some years ago, a taxi stopped for me, and just as the driver picked up my suitcase, he was intercepted by another driver who wanted the fare. Within minutes the two drivers were wrestling over my suitcase, exchanging blows and verbal abuse. After a doorman successfully intervened, and I was ensconced in the back of the first taxi, the driver began to tell me the story of his life. He spoke of the countless times life had been unfair, how he had been abused, how hard he had struggled to make a living, and how afraid he was of being taken advantage of. He spoke of the way that fear and resentment were part of his family culture, passed down through generations. The lineage of anger and suspicion goes back through time and generations, to a time before you were even born. If you could hear the unspoken, often hidden story of your enemies, you would find enough sorrow and despair in it to disarm all your rage and hatred.

There is little that is noble in suffering, but there is something deeply noble in our willingness to open to suffering without fear. If suffering were brought into being by choice, no one would suffer. Suffering is born not of choice or wisdom but of ignorance. One of the primary manifestations of ignorance is the belief in the solidity of self and other. The territory of self is defined by all that I feel I possess — my body, mind, my opinions, beliefs, religion. "Other" is defined by all that I believe you possess — your views, religion, race, gender, and history. Fear is the offspring of separation — the fear of loss, of threat, of challenge, and of deprivation. When anything of "mine" is threatened or even disagreed with, I feel the core of my being threatened. Nowhere is the sense of self and other more pressing and solid than in the midst of fear and anger. There is no ease, peace, or freedom in ignorance and separation. To find the end of suffering, you are asked to be relentless in your questioning of separation. Compassion is not built on sentiment but on wisdom.

Authentic compassion is altruistic, but it is not unrealistic. Walking the path of compassion, you are not asked to save all beings, lay down your life for another, or find a solution for all the problems in the world. You are asked to explore how you can transform your heart and mind in the moment. You are invited to turn toward the places in yourself where resentment, rage, and hatred live. With honesty, you examine your mechanisms of self-protection and defense to understand whether they truly preserve anything at all, apart from terror and isolation. To cultivate compassion and openness of heart in the midst of fear and pain is to swim against the current of the reactions that have been built up through your life. You cannot make yourself feel compassionate; trying to be compassionate always feels contrived. You also do not need to think of compassion as a random occurrence that takes you by surprise. Moment by moment, you can train your heart to open where it has previously been closed, to be intimate where you have sought distance.

Compassion is built on the foundations of tolerance, patience, forgiveness, and understanding. Nurturing a firm base of equanimity within, you find an inner balance that enables you to stay steady in the midst of life's storms. These foundations are not distant goals to be realized in some future time but truths that you can find and cultivate in the very midst of intolerance and fear. You do not need to wait for random moments when the walls that separate you from others crumble; you can learn to deconstruct the beliefs and cherishing that keep those walls solid.

A young man who worked with the homeless population of London said that every night, when he went out on the streets to do what he could to get people into shelters, to ensure that they had enough food, or to persuade them to come off their drug or alcohol habits, he hated it. Every night, he said, he met his own aversion and often the aversion of those he was meant to help. He often felt insulted when people spurned his advice, felt resentful when people turned down his offers of aid, felt judgmental when people preferred to huddle in a doorway rather than take up his assistance. After weeks, he said, going onto the streets at night was a journey into those corners of his heart he most wanted to avoid. Daily he would meet his own intolerance, impatience, and conditional generosity. Every night he met the division lodged in his heart between self and other. Every night was a journey of learn-ing patience and receptivity that he had never thought he was capa-ble of. Shantideva taught that it is our enemies that awaken our hearts.

Tolerance does not always come easily, but intolerance is no more than the habit of fear. You may be unconvinced that you can bear the loss and sorrow that life brings. The habit of protecting yourself against real or imagined danger and discomfort deepens. It is sometimes said that a quarter of the suffering in life is real and unavoidable, while the other three-quarters is born of trying to avoid the first quarter. None of us enjoys discomfort or difficulty, but the lengths we go to to avoid them are often greatly dispropor-tionate to the reality of the experience. We become increasingly intolerant as our fear of pain grows. We believe that we cannot endure a harsh word, a moment of disappointment, a fleeting hunger pang, a moment of distress. We flinch in the face of another's disapproval, avoid situations that threaten to disturb our hard-won composure. We are intolerant of boredom, believing that life should offer us endlessly interesting experiences. We believe that we're fragile and so approach life with trepidation and anxiety. When we lose faith in our own strength and fortitude, the world seems to be filled with danger.

If you are to find the vastness of heart that can embrace even the most dire situations of pain and cruelty, you must begin by addressing your relationship to the unpleasant. Wisdom and com-passion are not devices to fix your life, to ensure that you will be exposed to only pleasant people and events. We all have a certain measure of pain in this life. You are not asked to like it, but you are asked to learn what it means to remain steadfast in the midst of the difficult and the challenging. In the confusion born of fear, you can begin to believe that you are somehow entitled to be undisturbed. Your tolerance levels can be remarkably low, your capacity for forbearance subdued.

The training ground of compassion begins not with the demand that you embrace your worst enemies or your deepest fears but with the willingness to be still amidst the small transgressions and irritations that are part of all of our lives. You have to wait in line at the supermarket while the person in front of you redeems a wallet full of coupons, someone speaks to you in a scathing tone, your moment of relaxation is disturbed by someone intent on selling you something you don't want; someone keeps you waiting—life continues to offer countless possibilities for resentment. Often we don't want to accept even the possibility of being disturbed. Our sense of balance at times seems remarkably fragile, able to be shattered by any hint of the unpleasant.

You can dismiss these moments as irrelevant, but they are in fact the moments when you learn about equanimity and forbearance. Tolerance cannot be built overnight; like raising a child, it asks for perseverance and dedication, even in the face of tantrums and outrage. The places where equanimity and tolerance die most easily are the very places where you are asked to embrace and learn what tolerance truly is. Shantideva taught that there is nothing whatsoever that is not made easier through acquaintance, that by becoming acquainted with small harms you can learn to embrace greater harms.

Meditation practice is a training in tolerance, patience, and equanimity. You learn to sit like a mountain, to be still and receptive in all circumstances—happy or sad, healthy or sick. Your knee twinges or your mind is uncooperative, and you can sense the flight response arise—you want to run and abandon the difficulty. Yet, in those moments, you learn to embrace that reaction too, without being governed by it. In cultivating compassion you will be expected to encounter your fear of pain. You learn to be steadfast and still, understanding that the first building block of compassion is your simple willingness to keep showing up for all of life. That willingness teaches you that you won't be destroyed by your exposure to the difficult or unpleasant. You discover a genuine inner balance and sensitivity that can receive the difficult without being overwhelmed.

Equanimity and tolerance ask you to meet your own demons of aversion, self-righteousness, and prejudice. They are the demons that give birth to the hell realms, which erode confidence. You begin to see that each time you follow the pathways of aversion, flight, and resistance, you undermine your faith and confidence in yourself. You are telling yourself that you cannot tolerate this, that it is just too much to bear. Each moment you bolt from the reality or even the anticipation of the painful, you are building yet another fence that makes your world just a little smaller. You are telling yourself that your demons and the demons you meet in others are mightier than the vastness of your heart. If you tell yourself this often enough, you come to believe it, and the habits of fear and resistance can take over your heart and your life.

I once found myself standing in a parking lot with a friend who had historically carried a low tolerance threshold. He was engaged in well-worn litany of complaints about the idiocy of other drivers, the inconvenience of how the parking lot was mapped out, and the discourtesy of the people in the store we had been in. I found myself interrupting his tirade to ask him whether there was perhaps another way he could be responding to this mountain of perceived injustice. Looking bewildered he said, "None of this should be happening." Sometimes we are so accustomed to living in the house of intolerance and blame that we no longer even question it. We believe that, because we carry ancient traditions of resistance and impatience within ourselves, they will be with us until we die. The path of compassion asks us to overturn our habits, beliefs, opinions, and prejudices, to understand that our hearts can be transformed in every moment we are willing to be still, receptive, and aware.

You can take your meditation, your willingness to be still, into your life. You can learn to pause in the moments when you are prone to flee, to soften in the moments when you feel your heart hardening with resistance and blame. Cultivating tolerance is like opening the door to your heart. You might hope that only your friends come to visit, but you discover that your enemies too walk through that open door. Equanimity is a path you are learning to walk. Sometimes you open that door only slightly; that is all you can bear. Sometimes you stumble and slam the door, but your enemies and demons will wait for you. Just take your reflection upon tolerance into all the moments of your life, and see how it is for you when your heart can open and when it closes. Begin to investigate where the greatest suffering and harm are and where the greatest freedom and compassion are. With patience and tolerance, you learn to cross the borders of prejudice, fear, and resistance that divide you from yourself and from others. I once saw a street sign on which someone had written, beneath "stop," the words "being afraid."

The recipe for alienation is to support the opinions and prejudices that can deluge your heart. The recipe for compassion is the
willingness to continue showing up for your life and all it brings
to you. Compassion asks you to commit yourself to the end of suffering. You begin to discern not only what suffering is but what the
cause of suffering is. Seeing the fears and resistance that attach
themselves to the anxiety of "me," you see too that the healing of
suffering rests upon your willingness to no longer abandon anything in this world or in yourself.

David spoke of his journey from pain to compassion after discovering that his father had been sexually abusing David's young
daughter. David and his wife lived with a gnawing rage and anxiety for months after the discovery. Their children were given coun-
seling, and the parents were told of their children's deep-seated
trauma and fear. David needed to find a way toward healing without denying the atrocity. Attending his father's trial did little to calm
his rage, as he heard his father confess to numerous other incidents
of abuse. David's journey toward peace began with murderous
rage. He realized that in the rage he was capable of killing his own
father, and he also knew that he could not ever dismiss anyone who
acted out of a fury like he was feeling. His first step toward healing was to find the courage to speak about what he found unspeak-
able to those who could listen without flinching. Deep grief
followed, and then self-pity and pity for his daughters. He spoke
of a meditation session in which he felt that the ocean of his tears
was filled with everyone who had experienced loss through violence and abuse—Holocaust victims, street children, people in
Rwanda, and all the rest. Somehow the raw pain began to subside,
and he was able to be still in the grief. He acknowledged his need

to begin to "inch toward forgiveness." He reflected on his father's life now, imprisoned, shunned and banished from everyone he had ever felt affection for. David was able to feel the tragedy of this life, too. He said he needed to think of forgiving as an ongoing process rather than a static state. Forgiving, he said, was not only for himself and his father but for his own children and even the next generations. He began to work in restorative justice, a voluntary process in which perpetrators meet with their victims, offenders meet those they have harmed. The truth of harm can be spoken and listened to. Forgiving can begin.

Tolerance lays the foundation for turning toward the unbearable and unendurable. Compassion is born of your commitment to not bar anyone from your heart. Compassion in the midst of violence and brutality relies upon equanimity and understanding. It is a way of breaking the cycle of violence and hatred, and it begins with your willingness to be still. The great and small tragedies in your life and world sometimes just ask you to stand before them with silence and humility. You do not always have an answer, but you can learn to be present — listening deeply, with a heart that trembles in response to pain. Sometimes that is all you can do and all that you are asked to do. Compassion does not always bring an end to pain, but it can dissolve the suffering we layer upon pain with resistance and fear.

Tolerance needs to be rooted in wisdom. Just as the near enemies of compassion are pity and condescension, the near enemy of tolerance is endurance. A woman who had lived many years in an abusive relationship told me that her meditation practice had helped her to learn to bear an unacceptable relationship filled with cruelty. We can misuse meditation practice to avoid addressing the causes of suffering and finding the wise action to end those causes. Mistaking compassion for passivity just allows abuse to continue. Tolerance does not condone the unacceptable; learning to open to so much of the unnecessary suffering that scars our world is not the path we are asked to travel. We learn to find equanimity and inner balance so we can stay present with the painful inwardly and outwardly.

There are times when you can do little to alter pain and can only be still in its presence. There are also moments when opening to the painful and difficult is just the beginning of a path that also asks for the courage and sometimes fierceness of compassion. Just as you would pull a small child away from danger without rage or blame, so too you commit yourself to ending the causes of suffering without rage or blame. Again and again in your life, you are invited to ask yourself what is needed to ease the suffering of this moment. Do you need to say no when it is easier to say yes? Do you need to risk losing the approval and affirmation of others in order to speak or act with integrity? Do you need to do what is required rather than what is easiest? Do you need to go to the places that scare you and be willing to meet the anger or condemnation of others? Compassion is not a search for popularity but a commitment to honesty.

The Buddha spoke of the wisdom of cultivating clear intention in our lives. Recognizing that your intentions are the forerunners of your thoughts and actions, you can learn to tend to them with care and mindfulness. The arising of suffering and also the end of suffering begin with the intentions you bring to each moment of your life. The intentions of loving kindness and renunciation rescue you from their opposites—harshness and resistance. You can explore what difference it makes in your life to enter into each day and each moment with conscious intentionality. It means carefully attuning yourself to the rhythms of your heart and mind, moment to moment. Walk down the street and notice the places you open and the places you close. Notice what happens when a stranger smiles at you, and then what happens when you encounter a homeless person begging. Stay close to what happens in your mind when you meet someone who offends you.

Notice that in the absence of mindfulness you are driven by impulse and unconsciousness to close and defend. Compassion asks you to move from a life of reaction to a life in which you are mindful of your intentions. Be aware of the times you solidify resentment and bitterness by replaying your stories of what someone did to you. Explore the possibility of bringing loving kindness and the willingness to let go to all those moments. Ask yourself where you are choosing to make your home in each moment—in suffering or in the end of suffering. You can rescue yourself from division and alienation. The moments you do close down or become lost in outrage or blame are not moments of failure that warrant even more condemnation of yourself. You can compound suffering through self-blame or you can ask yourself what is truly needed to ease the contraction and fear. Through wise intention, you explore the possibilities of healing in the moment. You can only heal one moment of suffering and division at a time.

Compassion has no hierarchy of worthy and unworthy suffering; it makes no distinctions between the deserving and undeserving. Wherever there is suffering, there is a need for compassion. Finding compassion for those who cause pain is an ongoing practice requiring remarkable patience and perseverance. It is a difficult journey, but the path of bitterness and division is far more painful. The path of compassion begins with your willingness to soften and stay present in all the moments when you are prone to recoil and flinch. You learn to open your eyes and heart in all the places you have been blinded by fear or rage. You begin to dismantle the boundaries that have too long divided you from others.

GUIDED MEDITATION
Compassion for Those Who Cause Suffering

Create a dedicated space where you can be still and present. Allow your body to fully relax, allowing thoughts about the past and future to fade away. Take a moment to be intimate with your body, aware of all of the sensations that arise and pass. Feel your body touching the ground; be aware of the stillness of your body and the space around you. Let any places of holding or tightness soften and relax.

Let your heart begin to open to the vastness of affliction and suffering that pervades the landscape of life in this moment. Sense the countless beings around you who at this moment are living in danger, fear, and violence. Allow yourself to open to the person fleeing in terror from an advancing soldier as well as to the soldier holding the gun. Sense the heart of a person who trembles in fear in a torture cell and to the heart of the torturer. Let your heart embrace the child cowering before the threat of violence and the person raising her fist. Sense the grief of a person who has lost someone he loves to a drunken driver and to the person behind the wheel of the car. Let yourself open to the magnitude of pain that is part of the fabric of our world. Sense the trembling of your heart, and rest in that trembling. Allow the stories to fall away; allow your own fear and rage to rest in the quivering of your heart.

Let your attention rest in the simple intention to heal suffering.

> May you be free from fear and danger.
> May you be free from sorrow and pain.
> May you find healing.
> May you find peace.

If you are able to be still and open, bring your attention to those who cause pain — the abuser, the rapist, the oppressor, the offender. Allow the fullness of each person's being to emerge and rest in your attention. Sense not only their cruelty, selfishness, and violence but also their blindness, their panic, their ignorance, their terror. At times it is easier just to visualize them as a mass of darkness or density. Sense their fractured lives and hearts, their disconnection and alienation. Sense if it is possible for their pain and suffering to rest in your quivering heart. As much as you are able, extend to them the boundlessness of compassion.

> May you be free from fear and danger.
> May you find understanding and peace.
> May you find the way to healing.

Sometimes it feels like too much to ask of yourself to open to someone who creates sorrow and pain. Do not force it. Bring your attention back to your body, feel its stillness and the steadiness of your body's connection with the earth. Let your heart and mind calm. When you are ready, come back to what is difficult.

It may be important to make a connection with someone in your life who has harmed you or been a source of fear and danger. Again, begin by establishing yourself in stillness and steadiness. Extend a warm, compassionate attention to yourself.

> May I be free of fear and danger.
> May I be free from sorrow and pain.
> May I find peace and healing.

When you are ready, invite into your attention and heart someone you are alienated from or fearful of. As much as you are able, visualize or remember that person. As you hold the person in your attention, sense the responses that emerge in your heart and mind; know the fear, anger, or bitterness of that moment. Sense too the sheer painfulness of living in that fear and rage born of division and separation. See if it is possible to release the story of blame and resentment. Let yourself attend to the reality of suffering. Sense the suffering of that person's confusion and blindness and also their deep longing to be free of suffering, to be accepted, understood, and cared for. As much as you are able, even if it is only for a few moments, hold that person's pain in a heart of compassion.

> May you be free from fear and danger.
> May you be free from sorrow and pain.
> May you find healing.
> May you find peace.

Gently, bit by bit, you learn to approach the unapproachable, to open where you are prone to close. Moment by moment, you learn to nurture compassion where there has been division and terror. Step by step, you learn to ease suffering.

Compassion for Ourselves 5

THE BUDDHA ONCE SAID that you could search the whole world over and not find anyone more deserving of your love and compassion than yourself. When I first heard that, I was puzzled. Spiritual paths offer an abundance of teachings that stress selflessness, letting go of self-cherishing, and understanding the emptiness of self. Paradoxically, it seemed, here was a direct encouragement to cultivate love and compassion for myself. Reflecting on the Buddha's words more deeply, it is apparent that I could never extend a boundless compassion to anyone unless I know deeply what it means to hold myself in a compassionate heart.

Exploring your inner world, the relationships you form with all that arises in your body, heart, and mind, you discover a microcosmic view of the relationships you form with all life. Within this inner world, you sow the seeds of the compassionate heart or the alienated heart. In your relationship to your pain and sorrow, you cultivate the patience, forgiveness, and understanding that inform your relationship with all pain and sorrow. It would be naive to believe that profound compassion could be found to meet the great sorrow in life if you do not hold yourself in the same light. The training ground of boundless compassion is in all the small moments in which you meet the painful and difficult within your own life that you are prone to deny or reject. Compassion challenges the dualism of self and other. It is a heartfelt response to suffering as suffering, wherever it is found. "Your" suffering or "my" suffering are rendered meaningless by the wisdom of compassion. Suffering is just suffering.

Most of us find it easier to extend and feel compassion for others than for ourselves. We tend to treat ourselves with a level of harshness and demand that we would be reluctant to inflict on anyone else, even our worst enemies. We deny to ourselves the forgiveness, generosity, and patience that are at the heart of compassion, even as we intuitively acknowledge that they are essential to healing pain wherever it arises. Even as we open our hearts to others, to receive and embrace them, we habitually judge and condemn ourselves.

A friend was diagnosed with terminal pancreatic cancer and was told she had only six months to live. As the months went by, her weight plummeted, the pain increased daily, and she became too weak to get out of bed. She would accept only minimal doses of morphine, even as the pain became unbearable. The six months passed, and fifteen months later she was still alive, becoming more and more skeletal and weak. I asked her what was keeping her holding so tenaciously to a life that had become torture. She told me she wanted to die well, that she had done so much in her life that was wrong, and this last act of dying was one she wanted to do "right." When I asked her what it meant to die "right," she said she had to die without any fear or regret. She believed that her path demanded that she find the equanimity to overcome the pain and find the courage to face her death without flinching. Her sister remarked, "She is only willing to die if she can die a saint."

The burden of sainthood is a heavy one when your personal ideology equates sainthood with a perfection that denies your humanness. Compassion is made difficult when perfection is demanded. The error of equating liberation and compassion with perfection can make even dedicated people on a spiritual path into people who inflict extremes of violence upon themselves. Following the path of self-perfection, they heap suffering upon suffering and continue to be bewildered by the elusiveness of their ideals.

When I first began to practice meditation, one of the mostly unconscious motivations I brought to the path was the belief that a spiritual path was a more enlightened way of achieving the perfection I had sought in other dimensions of my life. I transferred lifelong patterns of self-blame and judgment into a new language and culture. I believed that if I could become more loving, peaceful, and wise, I would be worthy of enlightenment. It was in reality only a tired life view adorned in more spiritual language — the view that if I could become perfect and infallible, I would be worthy of love and acceptance. We can even find ourselves incorporating meditative and spiritual ideals into the portfolio of ways we punish ourselves. The tyranny of self-improvement brings harshness, judgment, and self-loathing that deny compassion.

We often alternate between the extremes of self-obsession and self-neglect. We tend to think far more about what we hate in our bodies, minds, and hearts than what we honor or respect. Limitless thought and preoccupation can be generated in the search to rid yourself of your failings and flaws, but it is an endless project.

You work on your anger, only to find it replaced by greed. Subduing your greed, you find the unwelcome appearance of pride. Ridding yourself of pride, you find some new flaw that requires yet more effort to subdue or annihilate it. What you hate in yourself you also fear. You think that unless you dedicate yourself wholeheartedly to the path of self-perfection, you will be overwhelmed by your flaws; you will be worthless. As Kabir put it:

> Friend, please tell me what I can do about this world
> I keep spinning out of myself!
>
> I gave up expensive clothes, and bought a robe
> But I noticed one day the cloth was well-woven.
>
> So I bought some burlap, but I still
> Throw it elegantly over my left shoulder.
>
> I stopped being a sexual elephant,
> And now I discover that I'm angry a lot.
>
> I finally gave up anger, and now I notice
> That I am greedy all day.
>
> I worked hard at dissolving the greed,
> And now I am proud of myself.
>
> When the mind wants to break its link with the world
> It still holds on to one thing.

Kabir says: Listen, my friend,
There are very few that find the path![1]

Should is a powerful word in the vocabulary of self-perfection. You "should" be more generous, courageous, loving, and balanced. Every "should" is a blow to acceptance and compassion. Every "should" undermines your capacity to open to the simple reality of pain and suffering — the acceptance that is the beginning of healing. Beneath the "shoulds" you can hear the lurking chorus of inner voices saying you are not good enough. The greatest obstacle to finding compassion for yourself is not the acts you regret or the pain or sorrow in your past or present but your tendency to harm yourself with self-denial and self-judgment. You harden your heart against yourself with an ongoing assault upon all that is human and fragile within yourself.

A young woman spoke of the crisis she faced after ten years of raising her severely autistic son alone. After the initial shock of his diagnosis, she dedicated her time and attention to her son so she could ease his isolation and suffering. One morning, she said, she woke up and felt she simply had no more to give. She began approaching her son with reluctance, going to bed at night with resentment, regretting the loss of the simple joys she saw in the lives of other mothers. She condemned herself for her failure to give her heart totally to her son. As the self-blame hardened, she found herself drowning in an ocean of rejection. She felt there was nowhere to go; her heart had turned to stone. Finally, she was able to simply embrace the suffering of the moment. She felt herself holding all the resentment, bitterness, and loss in a deep stillness. The judgment, blame, and anger were all threads of the same fabric of pain, all deserving of compassion. She began to sense that, as Thomas Merton, the Christian mystic, suggested, "true prayer begins in the moments when all doors are closed and our hearts have turned to stone." When we have exhausted all our strategies, told all the stories of blame, had our defenses overwhelmed, then it seems we can begin to open, to soften, and to sense the compassion that is needed.

We are often encouraged in meditative paths to let go of the tyranny of the inner judge. We would dearly love to do so, yet it is a pattern deeply rooted in family and cultural traditions and is often so automatic that we feel helpless before it. Self-judgment cannot exist without the forerunner of often-grandiose ideals and expectations that are hidden in the depths of our consciousness. Even the encouragement to let go of self-judgment can be translated into yet another demand and expectation, a sign of spiritual success or failure.

It might be useful to explore a different path, to become deeply curious about the mechanism of self-blame and denial. You can learn to be still and listen to the moments of greatest chaos and violence within your own mind. The pattern of self-condemnation does not ask for further resistance and blame but for mindful presence — this too is a song of your heart that merits your attention.

If you take just one day to listen to the litany of insults, criticisms, and judgments you heap upon yourself, you soon understand that the judgmental mind is without discrimination and without conscience. It will seize upon your successes as well as your failures, your appearance, your moments of happiness as well as sorrow. The judging mind is relentless in insisting that you should be someone other than who you are, and that all things and all moments should be something other than they are. Beneath the thoughts, you can begin to sense your personal beliefs and ideologies rooted in fear, shame, and an enduring belief in all that is broken within you rather than whole. The tendency to judge is a habit. You have walked the path of condemnation, and self-aversion so many times that it has become automatic. You sing the same songs of blame over and over. Each time you walk that path and heed those songs, you essentially reinforce the belief in your incompleteness and unworthiness. The need to bring the tenderness of compassion to all the places in yourself you have abandoned is not immediately apparent.

Thomas Merton once said that the essence of spiritual practice is "a search for truth that springs from love." That search begins when you have been absorbed in the fiction of your own brokenness and incompleteness. In the Sufi tradition it is said that, to discern what is true, not only your words but also your thoughts must pass through three gates. At the first gate you ask, "Is this true?" If it is, you let the thought pass through. At the second gate you ask of the thought, "Is this necessary?" If so, you embrace it. At the last gate you ask, "Is this rooted in love and kindness?" This last question is perhaps the most important. The habits of self-blame and judgment may be deeply rooted in your heart and history, but their perpetuation relies upon them remaining unattended to. The essence of mindfulness is to bring the light of attention to all that has been invisible and habitual. The purpose of mindful attention is to bring to all the moments of suffering and contraction the compassion that liberates your heart from pain.

As you begin to observe the judgmental mind, one of the first liberating insights is to see that judgment is a thought. It is a thought laden with aversion—for yourself, for others, for the simple truth of the moment. Blaming thoughts often carry the historical baggage of all the moments of disappointment, fear, and hurt you have encountered in your life. But just because these thoughts have been thought thousands of times before does not make them true; it simply reveals what you are most prone to seize hold of and believe in. Bringing an unflinching attention to these thoughts and judgments, you discover that when you are able to soften the aversion, judgmental thoughts have no foundation to sustain them. Thoughts are just thoughts. They arise and pass, appear and are released. They hold no intrinsic power to dictate the quality of your well-being.

Released from condemnation, you come to see that judgment, free of aversion, is an essential aspect of discriminating wisdom. The wisdom of compassion demands that you can discern what leads to suffering and what leads to the end of suffering. This capacity to discern is the forerunner of compassionate action. Aversion, whether for yourself, for another, or for anything in this world, is the proximate cause of disconnection and distance. Turning toward the rejecting mind, you begin to sense the pain of aversion and the sorrow of all the divisions born of aversion. As you turn your attention to the places where you are prone to disconnect, you are forging links of connection and relatedness. Compassion asks you to abandon no one and no thing in this world—including all the moments of recoil and harshness that are so difficult to face. In your willingness to be steadfast and present, the aversion begins to soften and melt. The alchemy of compassion has the power to bring a sense of possibility into all the moments and places that seem impossible. The Buddha was once asked by a disciple, "Would it be true to say that part of our practice is to develop loving kindness and compassion?" "No," he answered. "It would be true to say that the whole of our practice is to develop loving kindness and compassion."

Aversion for yourself, left unattended and unexplored, easily degenerates into one of the near enemies of compassion—self-pity. You recite your historical mantras toward yourself: *I'm a failure, unlovable, broken, incomplete; I can never change.* With each repetition, you descend further into helplessness and disconnection. Self-pity can also become a quality of self-absorption that serves to relieve you of having to investigate whether your labels and descriptions are actually true. The most lethal consequence of self-pity is that you are prone to settle for far less than what is possible. You come to believe that liberation, peace, and wholeness may be a reality for others but not for you.

Underlying compassion is the ethics of nonharming, which includes a commitment to cultivate an attitude of nonviolence toward your own heart, body, and mind. With mindfulness, you can learn to interrupt the habit of harshness toward yourself, manifested in self-blame and judgment. Instead of heedlessly traveling the old familiar pathways of blame and censure, you learn to open to the pain and treasure that pregnant pause of mindfulness. The slight gap between the arising of judgment and the contracting around it is where you can evoke compassion: *This too, this too.* The unconditional kindness of those pauses has the power to dissolve the underlying belief of unworthiness. The habit of aversion also calls for the fierceness of compassion. You can withdraw your consent from anything that adds to the mountain of pain, including the tendency to condemn or dismiss anything or anyone—including yourself. Ceasing to abandon yourself through judgment, you begin to explore the sadness, fear, and anger that lead you to abandon yourself. You begin to embrace the imperfect with compassion, to embrace yourself.

Acceptance is the forerunner of compassion, and intimacy is the forerunner of acceptance. The places where you are most prone to abandon yourself through judgment and blame are the very places you are asked to be most intimate with. As poet-songwriter Leonard Cohen said:

> Ring the bells that still can ring
> Forget your perfect offering
> There is a crack in everything
> That's how the light gets in[2]

If all were perfect in this world or in yourself, there would be no need for compassion. Acceptance is a process of letting go of your demand and insistence that life and yourself must be different than they are in this moment. This is not resignation but a deep inner willingness to embrace the imperfect in a heart free of judgment and blame. This willingness to open where you are most prone to close is a gesture of compassion in the service of ending sorrow.

The belief that you are unworthy of compassion can manifest not only in self-judgment but equally in self-abandonment. You look at the world with its immensity of pain and suffering and believe that your sorrows and difficulties are insignificant and unworthy of attention in the face of such dire suffering. You may even feel that it is somehow self-indulgent to care for your ailing body, your chaotic mind, or your broken heart. You can be wonderful at responding to and caring for others in pain but incapable of extending the same compassion to yourself.

Compassion that involves self-neglect is incomplete. Countless people and situations plead for your presence and care. Each day you meet the broken and fragile — the unbalanced person on the street ranting at invisible demons, ill and aging parents, heartbroken children. The path of compassion is to listen and respond, including to the quiet voice in your own heart. The belief that you are unworthy can manifest in a deafness toward your own being and an inability to draw the necessary boundaries to guard the balance of your heart. One of the near enemies of compassion is guilt and self-denial. You can care for the world in all your waking moments yet ignore the needs of your own heart and mind for compassionate attention. Boundaries can be born of fear but also of wisdom. It is important to know the difference between acts and words that come from love and those that come from guilt and self-denial.

Compassion listens to the cries of the world, and you are part of that world. As you walk a spiritual path, you begin to understand it is not about transcending yourself or sacrificing your humanness on the altar of some great ideal of achievement. You are always being asked to heal yourself. To know the pain, rage, and grief you carry in your own heart enables you to take your place on the path of all healing. A spiritual path asks you to find compassion for all the parts of yourself that are bitter, frustrated, and scarred by fear and rejection. Within all this sorrow, you learn the lessons of patience, acceptance, and, ultimately, of compassion.

Compassion for Your Body

Many spiritual paths appear to encourage a dismissal and neglect of the body. Images of emaciated saints occupy a central place on many altars. They transmit the message that a spiritual path demands transcendence of the body. At times the body is regarded as an obstacle, a problem to be overcome or ignored. In the early years of his practice, the young prince Siddhartha pursued a dis-embodied path of spirituality. He abused and ignored his body until he was near death. One day, as he was sitting on a river bank, weak and emaciated, a young woman came and offered him a dish of rice. Eating it and feeling his body respond to the nourishment was a turning point in his practice—a moment when he came back to a middle way and a path of balance. The Buddha encour-aged his students to find a middle path in their relationship to the body, neither neglecting nor gratifying it. He taught that by caring for the body it can become a vehicle for a deepening understand-ing of the path.

A path of compassion begins with the foundations of your expe-rience. You learn not to transcend your body but to be embodied, knowing that, as Walt Whitman once said, "Everything we do, have done or will do, we will do in our bodies." Your body can delight and torment you, it can be your ally and also seem to betray you. You suffer in your body, and some of the moments of deepest con-nection and intimacy are found through the body. Your body links you to all other bodies. If you are to awaken, to find a heart of com-passion, it too will be discovered while in this body. The compas-sion, loving kindness, and sensitivity that are nurtured on the path will be given life and expressed through your body.

It is perhaps no surprise that countless meditative practices begin with a contemplation of the body. We are asked to study our bodies, to be intimate with them moment to moment. This contemplation turns the tide of disconnection and fragmentation. We often live apart from our bodies, giving them attention only when they scream for it. As Al Huang said, "Many people treat their bodies as if they were rented from Hertz—something they are using to get around in but nothing they genuinely care about."

To contemplate your body is of course to contemplate the life of all bodies; the seasons of your body are the seasons of all life. You are born and die in your body. You encounter aging, sickness, and pain. Your sense of who you are is often deeply identified with your body and your appearance. The anxieties, confusions, struggles, and fear that arise in relationship to your body mirror the same patterns of disconnection that arise in countless other areas of your life. Your relationship to your body reflects your relationship to your mind and your world. Learning to find calmness, trust, and compassion within the world of your body, you learn to bring those qualities to all moments of life. In the contemplation of your body, you learn to weave together the relative and absolute worlds—caring for the world of form with bottomless integrity and compassion, yet not mistaking your body for the truth of who you are. You do not mistake the appearance of anyone or anything in the world for the truth of who they are.

We often either obsess about our bodies or ignore them. Compassion asks you to bring a respectful and mindful presence to your body, knowing it is a microcosm of all bodies. Intimacy is the key to compassion, and mindfulness is a practice that brings you ever closer to the simple truths of each moment. Being mindful of your body, you often discover layers of psychological, emotional, and spiritual wounds that have embedded themselves there. It is not unusual during intensive meditation retreats for people to find themselves sitting with intense pain, even though their postures may be relaxed and aligned. Even if meditation halls were filled with reclining chairs and masseurs, people would continue to encounter pain in their bodies, as they undertake the inner journey of exploring their lives. Fear, grief, and rage all make their home within our bodies, and these are awakened by the attention we bring to them in meditation. If healing and compassion are to awaken in your life, they will plant their roots in your body.

Some people treat pain as a personal failure, regard illness as weakness or as a signal of something they are doing wrong. It is easy to forget that many of the greatest spiritual masters have died of cancer, heart attacks, and strokes, just as the unenlightened do. We hate pain, and our response is often to flee from it or regard it as an enemy, an intruder that has stolen our well-being and happiness. When our bodies become ill or frail, the pain or illness becomes, through rejection, the "other," the opponent we have to endure or subdue. We believe that unless we succeed in quelling this other, we will be overwhelmed or overcome by it. Our deepest fears of being out of control are provoked to the surface. No one on a meditative path is asked to learn to like pain, but you are asked to learn what it means and not to become disembodied in the face of pain.

Your body, like all bodies, is fragile; it will age, get sick, and die. When you know this deeply and fully, you can begin to turn toward your body with compassion. Your body can communicate anger, fear, and disconnection, or it can communicate tenderness, kindness, and sensitivity. Knowing this can be a turning point in becoming fully embodied in your life. The life of your body mirrors and expresses the life of your heart and mind. You may never have the body you want or dream about, and the body you love and cherish may turn into one you no longer feel at home in. You may grieve over the loss of a body that was once vital and strong. The changes in the body bring with them lessons of compassion — touching the truth of the moment with patience and kindness.

A woman spoke of the way she sank into terror and loneliness in the days after she was diagnosed with breast cancer. She grieved over the potential loss of her femininity, the possibility of her children being left motherless, and the prospect of a future of pain, struggle, and death. After some days, she said, she realized she was misusing her imagination to terrorize her own heart, and the result was an overwhelming sense of helplessness and isolation. In those first days, she said, she found it nearly impossible to feel at home in her body. As part of her treatment, she attended a breast cancer clinic. The waiting and treatment rooms were filled with women, all with breast cancer. Some were young, some old, some in the early stages of treatment, and some near death. Being in the company of these women, she said, was humbling and opening. Curiously, the clinic became a place of sanctuary — no one tried to encourage anyone else to look forward to a better future, no one pretended that this great catastrophe wasn't happening, and she could put down the burden of reassuring others of her well-being. The honesty of the clinic stripped away pretense and in some strange stripped away terror. Fear, pain, and uncertainty remained, but it was a shared fear and uncertainty. Something that had at first felt impossible to be with or open to became possible. She said she ceased to think about it as *her* cancer, *her* pain, and even *her* breast.

She discovered in herself a new capacity for kindness, and her sense of helplessness was turned into a participation in her healing.

Spiritual teaching does not counsel you to deny, transcend, or annihilate anything in your life, nor will awakening or compassion erase any human experience. When you emerge from deep meditative experiences where you discovered profound insights, you need to embody those understandings in every area of your life. Awakening and compassion do not protect you from the changing events of your world or your life. Instead, you are asked to find the grace, balance, and understanding to be present in the world and in your body, free from clinging and grasping.

The source of suffering and fear is not your body; it is clinging. The obstacle to freedom and compassion is not the body; it is holding. It is just a short step from believing "I am my body" to believing "I am unlovable," "I am sickness," "I am pain." Releasing the tendency to mistake your body for your self releases the capacity to care fully for your body with mindfulness and compassion, without ever mistaking your body for the truth of who you are. It is a lesson in learning how to care for all bodies and forms with tenderness and understanding, without ever mistaking the world of appearance for the whole truth of anything. Wisdom asks you to see beneath the surface, beneath appearance; compassion asks you to embrace the flawed and imperfect and to treasure the well-being and harmony of all life, including yourself.

The Buddha taught that everything we need to understand can be understood within the length of this body. Within your body, you learn the lessons of change, suffering and the cause of suffering, and the path to the end of suffering. Within your body, you realize your capacity to bring patience, acceptance, and balance to fulfilment. Within your body, you learn to harmonize yourself with the seasons of life, the births and deaths that are intrinsic to living. Within your body, you explore what it means to let go and to realize the freedom and peace of that letting go.

The ethics of compassion ask you to live with a deep commitment to nonharming that extends to how you care for your body. Bodily acts of loving kindness describe not only the way you relate to the world around you, but the way you can learn to hold your body with all its strengths and frailties. You discover within all the changing seasons of your body a capacity to be present with equanimity and fearlessness. The fearlessness you learn to bring to the unpredictable world of your body does not imply that fear never arises but that you learn to stay steady, present, and open in the midst of fear.

Compassion for Your Mind

Many of us find it easier to find compassion for our bodies than for our minds and the minds of others. We live with the illusion that we should be in control of our thoughts and images, that we should be able to choose what thoughts appear. If you are willing to sit and contemplate your mind for even five minutes, you will quickly realize the absurdity of this notion. Contemplating your mind is akin to standing on a busy street corner: You hope that butterflies and birds will come along, but you are just as likely to get heavy trucks and exhaust fumes. You rarely get up in the morning and decide that this is a good day to be overwhelmed by obsession or mind storms. You don't leave home with the intention of spending your day irritated with the world, intent on dwelling on the past, or lost in fantasy. When you do get absorbed in confusion or obsession, it is easy to tell yourself you should know better, that your mind should be different than it is. When you meet other peoples' minds, the same intolerance tends to arise.

Your mind is marvellous storyteller, rarely at rest. You tell stories about yourself, about other people, and in fact about almost everything that enters your field of perception. At times, it seems as if your mind is on a mission to make everything in the world familiar and known. It is an exhausting mission. At the end of the first day of a meditation retreat, many people are amazed to find themselves so weary they can hardly keep their eyes open. All they have done all day is sit, but the constant stream of thoughts, imaginings, expectations, plans, and regrets consume a vast amount of energy.

A woman with an obsessive-compulsive disorder spoke of feeling tortured and imprisoned by her mind. Her thoughts governed her day, dictating her actions and her life. Before she could leave home, her mind would demand that she check three times that all her windows were closed, her oven turned off, her shoes aligned in a prescribed fashion. Her days were filled with rituals she longed to be free from, yet her demanding thoughts held more power than her longing to be free. She regarded her mind as an enemy; fantasy was the only escape from the incessant thinking that plagued her life. With mindfulness, she learned to soften her hatred of the obsessive thoughts, to replace resistance with curiosity, and their power began to wane.

It is a rare person who has not found his well-being shattered by the movements of their mind. Spiritual practice can be used as a way of suppressing thought, deepening our aversion to the mind. The mind becomes the focus of blame and denial and is treated as an obstacle. But mind has been given an undeserved bad press. The Buddha said, "Who is my enemy? My mind is my enemy. Who is my friend? My mind is my friend." He went on to say that meditation practice is a tool not to tame the mind but to train the mind. Meditation is not another device to manipulate or dismiss mind. It is a vehicle for understanding mind. With compassion, you come to see that your mind is as much in need of healing as any other dimension of life that is distressed or fevered.

There is great liberation in discovering that you can be mindful of your mind. There is great release in discovering that it is not thought that unbalances you but the authority that you give to thought. Through belief and confusion, you establish thought as the absolute determinant of who you believe yourself and others to be. You endow thought with the power to dictate your happiness and unhappiness through your belief in the stories you tell. Then you discover that you can, with mindfulness, step back from your stories, opinions, judgments, and conflicts, and in doing so you no longer define yourself or anything in the world by the contents of your mind. You learn to bring a compassionate attention into the heart of confusion and chaos, and it begins to calm. As with every dimension of compassion, making peace with your turbulent and at times fearful mind relies upon your willingness to be intimate with it.

You can learn to take care of your thoughts and let them be born of love, out of compassion for all beings. If you were to bring to just a single day the clear intention to be mindful of your thoughts, you would begin to sense which of your mind's patterns contribute to suffering and which contribute to the end of suffering. Being mindful of your thoughts, you discover that, like all things

that are born, they have ancestors. Your thoughts are born of feelings, beliefs, fears, and identity. With awareness, you are motivated
to look not only at your thoughts but at their foundations. The
alchemy of awareness is that it brings into the light of consciousness and attention all that has been hidden and unconscious. You
discover the discontent and anxiety that keeps your mind so busy
and occupied. These are the places that compassionate attention
can transform. You do not need to fix or manipulate. Compassionate attention is the first step on the road of letting go.

As your mind begins to calm, you also discover the creative
power of your thoughts to articulate insight and communicate
understanding. You learn to align your thoughts with your deepest values. You can investigate the birth and the cessation of sorrow.
Your mind can be an ally on the path of healing.

Compassion for Your Heart

Your emotional world is both personal and universal. As you open
to the rhythms of your heart, you meet a lifetime's accumulation
of sorrow, grief, and hurt. You encounter your capacity for rage,
resentment, harshness, and fear. You also meet your capacity for
tenderness, intimacy, and joy. The language of your emotions is
universal — grief, sadness, the longing to love and be loved, the
capacity to experience and to inflict hurt. The language of your
heart teaches you about your interconnectedness and your interdependence. You can reach out to someone who is grieving
because you know what grief is. You can comfort someone who is
hurt, fearful, or sad because you know the contours of those feelings in your own heart. You can hold another person's sorrow in

the tenderness of compassion because you know what it means to be held in the compassion of another.

We often hold dualistic views of our emotions. Some we deem to be shameful or unspiritual, and we strive to suppress or overcome them. Other emotions we value as positive, worthy of pursuit, and we strive to gain or maintain them. The first step in healing your heart is to be willing to put down the dualism. Compassion by nature is unconditional, embracing all suffering. You are asked simply to be still in the face of powerful emotions. You can learn to be emotionally awake and greet those emotions with the same depth of listening and sensitivity with which you would greet any suffering and pain in the world.

You are asked to learn the lessons of patience, kindness, and acceptance again and again. Difficult emotions do not disappear through will or because you don't like them. Healing does not have a timetable. Ram Dass once said, "You cannot open to something in the hope that it will go away, because it knows." You are asked to be present with all the waves of pain, sorrow, and fear that appear. Each time, you are asked to listen and meet those waves as if for the first time. Your heart can be broken many times in your life. Your broken heart can also be healed over and over. If you were to ask yourself what you truly needed in any moment of heartache, the answer would be "compassion." The path of awakening the heart teaches that you can extend compassion to yourself.

An awakened heart feels deeply, loves well, and treasures forgiveness. The creative potential of your emotions to cross the boundaries between self and other is released as you discover what it means to be no longer imprisoned in emotional chaos and confusion but to rest in emotional wakefulness. You can learn to let go of stories and conclusions and open to the life of your heart and all hearts. As the poet Rumi once said, "The only lasting beauty is the beauty of the heart."

GUIDED MEDITATION
Compassion for Yourself

Find a posture in which you can relax and be still. Take a few moments to attend to your body, consciously softening any areas where there is tension or holding. Take a few slightly fuller breaths, with each out breath allowing your mind and body to increasingly relax and soften. With each out breath, release any agitation within your mind. Allow your attention to settle fully within your body and your breath.

Take a few moments to be aware of the life of your body — how it has been in the past, how it is now in the present, and how it may be in the future. Sense how your body holds all the seasons of life — birth, aging, and death. Reflect on the joy and delight you have found within and through your body. Reflect too on the pain, frailty, and illness that is also part of your body's life. Take a moment to reflect on the painfulness of the fear, resistance, and blame you can bring to your body as it goes through its changes. As you open to the life of your body, sense how you are exploring and connecting with the life of all bodies.

Sense whether it is possible to hold the pain, frailty, and aging of your body within a compassionate attention that is free of blame and rejection. If there is any area of your body that is painful or ill at this moment, bring your attention directly to that place of pain, without demand or fear. Offer to your body the compassion that can embrace all struggle and suffering.

> May I find healing.
> May I find peace.
> May I find openness of heart.

As you are present, allow the stories of your body, your fears of the future, to soften and be still. Sense any waves of resistance or aversion for your body that appear. Let them too be held within compassionate attention, rejecting nothing, embracing your body and your relationship to your body with an unconditional tenderness and care.

> May I find stillness within change.
> May I find the acceptance that allows me to be present
>   in this body.
> May my body be at peace.

Allow your attention to expand to embrace the life of your mind in all the ways that you experience it. The times of confusion and chaos, the moments of stillness and calm, the times of obsession and anxiety, the moments of ease and wisdom—let them all be held within a compassionate attention. Sense the moments when your mind seems to be lost within cascades of judgment and blame. Sense too the moments when your mind is an ally and a refuge. Release the blame, the insistence, the demand that you place upon your mind. Sense deeply the great pain and sorrow of a mind not at ease with itself, the torment of being lost in confusion.

Offer to yourself the compassionate attention that rejects nothing, that is free of blame—the compassion that can receive all sorrow.

May my mind find peace.
May my mind be at ease.
May my mind be safe and protected.

Allow your attention to expand to embrace the life of your heart. Reflect on the boundless sorrow you can feel in your heart, the world of loneliness, fear, grief, rage, jealousy, loss, and mistrust. Sense too the moments of joy your heart delights in—intimacy, love, tenderness, appreciation, generosity. Be aware of the need to bring compassion into all the moments of turmoil and darkness your heart can hold. Offer to yourself, bring into your heart, the compassion that has no boundaries, that can embrace all sorrow.

May I find healing.
May I find the willingness to embrace all pain.
May I find peace in all moments.

Moment by moment, open into the places you are prone to flee from or deny within your own body, mind, and heart. Receive the life you are living with a heart of compassion. Soften into the healing that is possible in this moment. Rest in a compassion boundless enough to embrace all sorrow.

Compassion for Those We Love 6

O N LEARNING of their mother's inoperable cancer and her impending death, a family gathered and agreed that their last gift to her would be to shield her from knowing the truth about her condition. As she lay in the hospital, each day gradually fading away, she struggled with pain and fear. Each day, her family assured her she would soon be going home, feeling better, on her feet again. They surrounded their mother with love and also with mythology. After their mother's death, their grieving was made more acute by knowing they had deprived themselves of the last precious chance to open to their mother, to communicate to her all that they held in their hearts, and to say good-bye. They also carried the pain of knowing that they had, in their wish to be kind, deprived their mother of the opportunity to meet her death as she may have wished.

All of us have moments in our lives when our hearts are touched and broken by the sorrow and pain of those we deeply love and care for. Parents sit by the bedside of their child as she undergoes yet another debilitating cycle of chemotherapy. A husband watches his wife's descent into alcoholism and depression that places her beyond his reach. Your parents will age and become frail; your partner and dearest friends will experience their own measure of misfortune and pain. In all those moments of sorrow, those you love may reach out to you, asking for your presence, your compassion, your wisdom. You are asked to be fearless where there is fear, to be steadfast where there is wavering, to be open in the face of resistance and denial. You heart can be broken in the face of a loved one's pain, and your heart can also be broken open.

Your capacity for forbearance, patience, and courage is most sorely tested when you are faced with a loved one's pain that you cannot fix or heal. To be human is to form bonds of intimacy. An intrinsic part of those bonds is the reality that you will be asked to open yourself to separation and helplessness. Instinctively, you reach out to shield your loved ones from pain, to protect them from hurt, but life continues to teach you that your power has limits. Compassion asks you to act with wisdom to relieve suffering whenever possible and equally to embrace the limits of your agency and power.

In your closest and most intimate relationships, attachment is the near enemy of compassion. It is not the attachment itself or the deep bonds of care that sabotage compassion and wisdom. It is your desire to control all things, including pain, that undermines compassion. It is your insistence that impermanence should never touch you or those you love. You get lost in the belief that your love should be powerful enough to protect those you love from suffering. Then you discover that it is not. Panic and anxiety can arise with that discovery; so too can a heart that is boundless in its compassion.

If you are lost in your insistence that life must be other than it is right now, you disempower your capacity to bring compassion and healing to the moments of pain you inevitably meet. You can acknowledge that you deeply wish that your child, parent, or friend were not suffering. Honoring that heartfelt wish is the seed of compassion, which grows through your attention. You yearn for a loved one's solace and ease. You can explore what it means to bring that wish into the midst of suffering and open to the reality of what is present. Those same longings and intentions can also be turned into insistence and denial. When you turn away from the sorrow and pain you feel you cannot bear, you deny not only a loved one's pain but also the truth of their experience. To be a refuge for another, you must remain connected with the truth of their pain and remain unflinching in the face of that truth.

When a loved one is ill, in pain, or dying, you might tell yourself that it is better to protect them from reality. You might find yourself speaking of better, future moments, when the pain has ended. But you can compound their fear with your agitation and refusal to address the simple truth of the moment. Fear often appears simultaneously with pain. It can arise when you face an uncertain future or the prospect of loss and death. That fear does not ask for judgment or dismissal, nor does it ask for denial or pretense. Your fear is part of the tapestry of suffering. It asks for your compassion and tenderness.

A nurse in a children's hospice had in her care a young girl in the end stages of cancer. Most of the time the child rested pain-free in her hospital bed, in the nurse's words, "curiously calm and also most introspective." When her parents came to sit with her, her mood would often change into restlessness and petulance. The parents then would withdraw from their child or lecture the nurses on doing more to ease her pain. As the hospice staff began to speak with the parents about the deep fear, anger, and panic they were experiencing, they came to realize that their beloved child was reflecting their own confusion and distress. Their daughter was try-ing to hold on to life to ease her parents' grief and their reluctance to let her go. It was as if fear and grief prevented them from par-ticipating in the process of her dying. As they began to understand this, they were more and more able to sit with their daughter with-out anxiety and enter into her calmness. The family was able to spend their last days and hours together in a shared love.

Life is an ongoing teaching in letting go. The Dalai Lama, in offering a teaching on impermanence, invited students to reflect on "what could disappear." We could expand that exploration to reflect on what has disappeared and what is now disappearing. Can you find anyone or anything in your life that is exempt from dis-appearance? Reflect on what has already disappeared: your infancy, childhood, adolescence, and all the joys and sorrows they held; the countless experiences of praise and blame, success and failure, pleasure and pain of your past. All your experiences of sounds, thoughts, sights, and feelings have faded into the past. There are people you have loved who are no longer part of your life, trau-mas you have healed from, aspirations and ambitions you no longer yearn for. Some of what has disappeared you grieve for, some you rejoice in. We welcome the truth of impermanence when it means the disappearance of something or someone we abhor. We struggle with change most deeply when it deprives us of the things and people we cherish, and most of all when it defies our attempts to control life. Whether you grieve or rejoice makes little difference to the reality that life always changes. All that arises will pass, all that is born will die, all that appears will disappear.

It is wise to reflect on all that will disappear. The goals and longings that feel so urgent at this moment will change or be replaced
by others. Everything that you define as being yours will pass. Your
body, your possessions, all that you rely on and love are part of the
rhythm of change. Your friends and your enemies, those you love
and those you despise, your moments of tragedy and your
moments of glory, all will pass. Reflect on what is disappearing at
this very moment. The thought that seemed so urgent is replaced
by an equally demanding one; the compelling feeling of sadness
is already changing into something else; the sound you delighted
in is already fading. Your body, mind, and world is changing
moment to moment.

The acute awareness of change, of appearance and disappearance, can terrify you into retreating into control and anxiety. It can
lead you to curb your willingness to love, for fear of loss and
heartache. But the profound understanding of impermanence can
also liberate your heart. You can love with grace and wisdom, in
the full understanding that love is also letting go. Liberating your
heart from the fear of disappearance and from the insistence that
nothing should change in a deep way also liberates all the people
in your life. They are freed from your demand that they should
never suffer or depart.

The encouragement of all spiritual paths to embrace the non-
negotiable reality of change is not a teaching of indifference or dis-
regard. It is a teaching that invites you to understand that whenever
you live in a way that is not in accord with life's essential realities,
you will suffer and compound the suffering that is already present. Love is easily distorted by attachment and demand. You may

feel that your love alone should be able to save your loved ones from being touched and saddened by life's changes. You may feel that love should protect you from loss and sorrow. When love does not embrace the wisdom of impermanence, birth and death, it is rooted in a denial that will break your heart and shatter your capacity to be a compassionate refuge for those you love.

Letting go is not a relinquishment of love but a release of illusion — the illusion that love will protect you and your loved ones from life's natural rhythms. Aachan Cha, a Thai forest master, once said that "if we let go a little, we will find a little peace; if we let go a lot, we will find a lot of peace; and if we let go completely, we will discover complete peace." Your whole life, everything that has appeared and disappeared in it, has been teaching you the art of letting go. It is a teaching of peace and freedom. It is also a teaching that runs counter to our tendency to want to choreograph and direct all the things in our lives. Perhaps nowhere do these tendencies arise more powerfully than in our relationships to those we love and treasure. We fear their loss, and we fear that we will be unable to bear our own heartache. Being patiently willing to cultivate the art of letting go in the places we hold most tightly brings a freedom from fear and resistance.

It is said that the most direct way to transformation and freedom is to turn toward the very places and experiences you are most prone to abandon. Compassion in its deepest sense is the practice of nonabandonment. Your most intimate relationships are the places where love and fear can grow simultaneously. You may believe it is the depth of your love that makes you fear its loss, but it is not love that brings fear — it is the demand that your love should be the only thing in this world that is exempt from change.

Resistance to loss can also make your heart wither. Fear makes you self-centered and self-preoccupied. You retreat into a separate self, fearing the invasion of reality and change. In that withdrawal, you too often separate yourself from the very person you love and are trying to protect. Fear has created an abyss, a separation between self and other that feels uncrossable. It is love, rooted in a deep understanding of the nature of life and change, that heals that divide. The power of compassion lies in its capacity to dissolve the separation between me and you. It is no longer your suffering or my suffering but just suffering. It is no longer your fear or my fear, but a fear of groundlessness that is universal. There is no freedom in pretending that groundlessness is not real. There is profound liberation in releasing yourself from mythology and taking refuge in the truth that you simply cannot control the way that life unfolds.

Letting go is not a destination but a process and a life path. You will not have one dramatic, transcendent moment of letting go and then be able to retire. Life will continue to present you with moments of pain, fear, and loss. They are all moments that will ask you to reach deeply within yourself to find your capacity for compassion and wisdom. Each moment you find yourself trying to control the world is a moment you are asked to reflect on what it means to let go. Each moment you find yourself retreating into fear and resistance is a moment that invites you to find the freedom of letting go. Each time you find yourself abandoning the pain or sorrow before you is a moment you are asked to come back. Your capacity to let go in those moments does not diminish your capacity to love and care — it liberates you to be wholeheartedly present in the face of pain without flinching.

If you are to be fully present with a loved one when they suffer, you must make peace with your own sense of grief and powerlessness. To be fearless does not mean that fear will never arise. A compassionate heart learns to embrace the fear instead of fleeing from it. After a house fire in which their daughter was badly burned, the parents, who had escaped unhurt, sat beside their child in the intensive care unit, day after day. At first they were almost unable to look at their once-beautiful child, whose body and face were now almost unrecognizable. It was, they said, "beyond bearing" to listen to her cries of pain when the morphine began to wear off. They sat too with endless waves of guilt, asking themselves over and over what more they could have done to save her and why only they should have been spared. For weeks, guilt, aversion, and fear were their world. With help, they began to see the interwoven strands of the anguish; their pain and their daughter's suffering were not separate. They also began to understand that if they were to be truly present for their child and a part of her recovery, they would all need to heal together. The tendency to abandon casts its shadow equally on all things. If you abandon your own fears of loss and resistance to change, the same tendency to abandon will distort your capacity to bring compassion to those you love.

Love asks you to let go; compassion asks you to let go. Your capacity to be wholeheartedly present for anyone or anything in this world asks you to release your longing for how things used to be and your yearning for a better future. Letting go frees you to take your seat firmly in this moment and in the truth of loss and change. Letting go frees you of the burden of obsessing about what used to be and what might be in the future. Your willingness to let go of what "should be" liberates you to embrace what is. This is one of the hardest of all lessons for us to learn and the lesson that none of us can avoid in this life.

The Buddha endlessly encouraged his disciples to take their seats and reflect upon the futility and suffering born of clinging. He counseled his students to take into their hearts these reflections: Can there be clinging without pain? Can freedom and clinging coexist? What does it mean to let go? He encouraged them to turn these reflections to all the places in their lives where clinging and resistance were found—their past and future, their bodies and minds, their longings and fears, and even the people they loved most deeply. Most of us, when we engage in these reflections, discover that the places we resist and cling to most tenaciously are also the places we suffer most acutely. They are the places we feel most imprisoned in a world governed by self and disconnected from others. Compassion is a release from that imprisonment and a healer of separation. Letting go does not leave you marooned in indifference or apathy; you are not asked to let go of your love or bonds of commitment and care. You are learning, step by step, moment by moment, to let go of suffering and separation. Your capacity to find a boundless compassion is released by your capacity to let go.

You learn the kindness of compassion in the places in your life where resistance registers most powerfully. Faced with the heartache, illness, or impending death of a loved one, you can anticipate that resistance will surge within you. The body tightens and the mind freezes, as you search for solutions and in many ways disconnect from the sorrow and suffering of the moment. You turn yourself into a helper, a healer, or even a saviour, sometimes forgetting that what the person before you most needs in that moment is your heartfelt presence. You can learn to spot the signals of resistance in your body, mind, and heart and understand that these are invitations to soften, open, and let go. Suffering does not require answers, explanations, or solutions. Instead it pleads for your sustained connection and openness. There is great wisdom in learning how to soften. You come to see that in resisting pain, death, and sorrow you are resisting life itself.

Loss is a rocky and unpredictable landscape that you often enter without a map or guide. When you are faced with the illness, impending death, or heartache of a loved one, you may find yourself going through stages of loss. These stages of loss are also the stages of learning to let go. Typically, you enter the territory of denial, the harshness of anger, the agitation of trying to negotiate with reality, and the darkness of depression. There will also be moments of grace and acceptance. There is no linear path in moving through loss. You are only asked to be patient, steadfast, and gentle with yourself and those around you. You are learning to embrace the most challenging truths of your life, and it is not easy.

Denial is often the first expression of fear and doubt. Watching their mother descend into the fog and confusion of Alzheimer's, her grown children collectively yet nonverbally agreed to pretend it was not happening. A little forgetfulness, they told each other; momentary lapses, they told her. As their once independent, strong parent increasingly declined, their denial also increased. When the truth became inescapable, they were asked to face their loss. The mother they had relied upon for so much was turning into a very different woman, almost a stranger, who now needed someone to rely upon. They feared they would be unable to care for her and doubted their capacity to embrace their own pain. They spoke of the loss of certainty in their world, caused, it seemed, by their mother's illness. Their image of her as reliable, available, and loving was being shattered. So too were their images of themselves, as children held within a safe and ordered world.

Upheavals in your life, born of changes in those you love, invite and even demand that you change to meet new realities that you do not always feel prepared to meet. Outer change invites inner change; inner change invites outer change. Whenever you stubbornly cling to a position, attached to how things used to be, you deny to yourself the life that is possible in this moment. It takes great courage to embrace the changes that life is constantly presenting. Resistance is the alternative, and in resistance you suffer and set yourself apart from the simple truths of the moment.

It is the reluctance to meet new realities, born of tragedy, loss, and change that can lead us to feel so angered by change. Facing the heartache, illness or pain of a loved one, you may find yourself regressing into familiar childhood mantras: "It's not fair, this shouldn't be happening." Anger makes you feel that the sorrow and pain in your life is somehow unjust. Storms of blame can follow in the wake of feelings of impotence and helplessness. You blame God, the medical profession, yourself; your blame has no discrimination or conscience. Storms of anger are deeply painful, like a forest fire that consumes everything in its path. Anger isolates and consumes the very compassion that can bring serenity and calm to the places of suffering. Anger is not calmed by heaping judgment or self-blame upon it. Anger is part of learning to open to the realities of birth and death, beginnings and endings, the unarguable uncertainty of all life. You can learn to soften within the tight bands of anger that bind you, bring compassion to the storms of blame that can deluge your mind, and simply be present with the sorrow of loss.

If left unattended, the impetus of anger often turns into an agitated endeavor to negotiate your way out of suffering. You make vows to change your life, be a better person, be more saintly, as a way of trying to stem the tide of loss. Like building a dike from sand to hold back a rising sea, you bargain with life to try to grasp the ungraspable. Your negotiations and bargaining, the busyness of trying to find a solution to suffering, become a cloak, armoring you against feeling the pain of letting go. Busyness can also exhaust you, depleting the energy, mindfulness, and presence that is needed to embrace sorrow without being overwhelmed.

As you discover that your efforts to alter the pain of a loved one are impotent, you are liable to sink into despair. Within the fabric of despair lies a sense of failure. Your efforts to fix or save a loved one from pain or sorrow have borne no result; they still suffer. You have reached the end of the journey of doing.

This is a critical point in the path of compassion. You can remain stuck in an exhausted despondency or sense the beginnings of acceptance. You can learn in those moments what it means to begin to release the role of the doer, the saviour, and be simply present with the pain of the moment and the peace of letting go of all your demands of how life should be. You face your own vulnerability and the vulnerability of all life, including those you love most dearly. You learn that the impotence of your agency does not reduce you to powerlessness. You discover within yourself the power to be present, to listen deeply, and to embrace sorrow in a heart of compassion. You do not have to be anyone special to take your seat in the midst of pain with openness, patience, and courage. If you are willing to turn toward the places you most wish to flee from, you can be surprised by the rich veins of steadfastness, acceptance, and kindness that lie beneath the veneer of your fears and resistance.

Acceptance is not passive or resigned. Acceptance has many layers. It begins with the willingness to embrace the simple truth of the moment: This is suffering, this is pain, this is loss, this is fear. You surrender the desperate yearning and search for a happy ending, and your heart and mind begin to calm and settle into a new-found stillness. Acceptance means you find the willingness to embrace the endings that are part of all our lives. In facing the death or heartache of a loved one, you embrace your own dying and heartache. Acceptance is the beginning of peace. It holds within it the possibility of a new understanding of compassion. You find within yourself the capacity to be wholeheartedly present in the face of pain, to listen deeply. You learn to be a little emptier inwardly, as you liberate yourself from the agitation of fear, demand, and insistence. You discover that the separation between yourself and another, born of fear and resistance, begins to dissolve. You do not have to try to be compassionate. You are simply asked to clear away the obstacles so compassion can emerge.

GUIDED MEDITATION
Compassion for Those We Love

Sitting comfortably in a relaxed posture, allow your eyes to close and your body to soften. Take some moments to notice any areas of your body where there is tension or holding, and let them soften. Be aware of the life and vitality of your body within the stillness of your posture. Sense the different sensations that appear and disappear. Notice how your mind is in this moment. Does it feel agitated, anxious, or heavy? Be aware, without judgment, of any thoughts or images that are registering in your mind. Sense how the thoughts arise and pass, appear and fade, begin and end. Take a few moments to listen wholeheartedly to the sounds of the moment, noticing their beginnings and endings, their birth and death. Sense deeply the way in which beginnings and endings, births and deaths, are part of each moment. Be aware of what happens in your body, mind, and heart if you try to reach out and hold on to or maintain any single sound, thought, or feeling. Feel the tightening, the hardening, that follows in the wake of any effort to control the uncontrollable or grasp the ungraspable. Feel too the softening and ease that follows in the wake of a willingness to allow endings to naturally following beginnings, the calmness that is born of your willingness to be present and to let go. Sense the way each moment in your life is a classroom in which you learn about the causes of suffering and the causes of peace.

Bring your attention back to the stillness and ease of your body, and let your attention settle in the center of your chest, in the area of your heart. Invite into your attention, into your heart, someone whom you love dearly, who is at this moment well. Reflect on the seasons of life that will touch that person, the changes they will be asked to meet. Know that you will be asked to witness and be present with that person in a time of pain, heartache, illness, or death. Allow yourself to feel the sadness of inevitable loss. Feel too the resistance, the fear, the anger that may come. Allow yourself to embrace the whole spectrum of feelings, denying none of them.

Sense the possibility of touching the spaciousness and grace, the wisdom and compassion, that may emerge.

Invite into your heart and your attention someone you care for deeply who is in pain, suffering, or sorrow. Visualize the person's face, the circumstances of their life right now. Allow yourself to feel their pain, heartache, despair, loneliness, or fear. Feel deeply too your own response, without blame. Sense the way in which you may wish to push away the reality of pain. Sense the grief that is part of loving, and sense too the anger or fear that may not be part of caring.

Offer to your beloved your heartfelt wishes for their well-being and peace.

> May you find peace.
> May you find ease in your heart.

Let your attention rest calmly, over and over again, in those heartfelt wishes.

> May you find peace.
> May you find ease in your heart.

Bring your attention back to your own heart. Sense the waves of sadness and sorrow that may be there, allow yourself to explore the landscape of grief and of letting go. Offer to yourself your heartfelt wishes for your own well-being and peace.

> May I find stillness in the midst of change.
> May I find peace in the midst of struggle.

May I find softness in the midst of resistance.
May I rest in compassion.

Allow your attention to alternate between the loved one and yourself, sensing the interwoven threads of pain and of love. Do not try to make yourself feel anything special. Compassion in this moment is not a specific feeling but a willingness to open without conditions to the tapestry of pain. Compassion is your willingness to be present, to listen deeply, and to hold sorrow in the vastness of your heart. Come back to the practice in all the moments you find yourself lost in struggle, despair, or fear. Sense the possibility of creating a refuge in your heart for yourself and for those you love most deeply.

Compassion in Adversity 7

A N ELDERLY MONK found his way to Dharamsala in India after twenty years of imprisonment. Meeting with the Dalai Lama, he told his story, recounting the years of torture, brutality, and isolation. Then the Dalai Lama asked the monk, "Was there a time you felt that your life was truly in danger?" The old monk answered, "The only times I felt deeply endangered were the moments I felt in danger of losing my compassion for my jailers." This is a story of a profound commitment to compassion, a story of faith and forbearance that bears witness to a human being's dedication to keeping his heart and dignity intact in the face of the greatest adversity. The stooped, wrinkled old monk was a simple man without credentials, education, or sophistication. He was also a man with a remarkable heart, who had chosen to forsake the pathways of bitterness and rage, knowing that in following those ways he risked losing what was most precious to him — the home he had made in compassion.

You may never face such extreme adversity in your own life, but you are certain to meet countless moments of hurt, rejection, criticism, blame, and aversion. You may have enemies, the people you have cast out of your heart through fear and bitterness. You will inevitably find yourself in situations where your heart is injured by the words and acts of another. If you were to reflect back on your life, you might see that it is often not the many acts of kindness and tenderness you have received that have made the deepest impression on your heart, but moments of ridicule, blame, insult, and hurt. Playground snubs, rejection by those you love, disapproval when you crave approval, and injured pride are part of all our lives, and they make powerful imprints. Too often we find ourselves thinking and even obsessing more about those who have harmed us than about those we love. It's as if we cherish the moments of hurt, making pilgrimages to revisit them, over and over, as if they were holy shrines. Each visit is painful, yet we find it so difficult to release the hurt. It is within this territory of injury and hurt that a fortress of bitterness and anger can be built. In the midst of the adversity in your own life, you too will be asked to choose which pathway you will walk—bitterness and rage or compassion and forgiveness.

Resentment and joy, hatred and love, bitterness and compassion are the outcome of what you cultivate and nourish. Nurturing compassion does not mean pursuing a quiet mind, isolated and divorced from anything unpleasant or difficult. If every word you heard was agreeable, every action kind, and every person flattering, you would perhaps have an agreeable mind but also a mind lacking in depth and vitality. Compassion is nurtured in the moments of adversity. It is in difficulty that you are invited to notice what you are cultivating. What you nurture will shape your mind.

One of the core teachings of the Buddha is that what you dwell upon becomes the shape of your mind. The shape of your mind determines how you perceive the world and how you engage and interact with that world. If you cherish the seeds of bitterness, fear, and resentment, your world becomes filled with enemies. Each moment you spend cherishing rancor and rage is a moment in which you are increasing your propensity for anger and bitterness. The next time you meet someone or something that irritates or offends you, you will find it just a bit easier to become lost in rage and resentment.

You might find yourself building walls of defense to keep your enemies at bay and armoring your heart to protect it from injury. In such a lonely and isolated life, you settle for far less that what is possible. Protection is always a poor substitute for a genuine sense of connectedness. Fear is a denial of faith, a repudiation of the confidence that you can discover within your heart the steadfastness and balance that enables you to meet your world with compassion. If you are to reclaim your heart, you are asked to explore what is needed to heal the places of rage and bitterness that feel most embedded and solid. The anger and blame that so agitates our minds are often a camouflage cloaking feelings that we judge as too terrible to experience directly — hurt and fear.

The first step on the path of compassion lies in your willingness to turn your attention directly to the experience of anger and bitterness. Take a moment to invite into your heart just a single memory of being harmed or a single person you are in conflict with. You will feel your body tighten in resistance. You will feel your mind begin to replay the story of hurt, humiliation, or rejection, in an endless loop. You will feel your heart surge with fear or resentment. The person who harmed you may be long removed from your life, yet he or she has been given a permanent address in your heart. You continue to breathe life into the hurt by dwelling upon it. As you are willing to explore the landscape of hurt, fear, or resentment, you discover that you are now suffering more from your anger and bitterness than from the acts that originally aggrieved you. You begin to directly experience the truth of Shantideva's words: "My mind will not experience peace if it fosters painful thoughts of hatred. I shall find no joy or happiness. Unable to sleep, I shall feel endlessly unsettled." Understanding this, you begin to sense that the healing you long for will not be born of revenging yourself upon your enemies but will begin in your own heart.

What you meet in that landscape of bitterness is an injured self-image. Your sense of who you think you are has been violated. You have been denied the respect and care you sought. You may feel that you have been disempowered or debased by another person or that your self-respect or self-worth has been damaged. Whether anyone or anything in this world truly has the power to do these things is a question that rarely arises. The pain and anger in your heart disables your capacity to grant yourself the well-being, respect, and tenderness you long for. The injured self is invariably an agitated self, and the agitation is fueled by dwelling in anger and bitterness. You may find yourself replaying conversations of hurt and rehearsing the exchange you wish to have in the future. You play long inner monologues of self-justification and nurse your injured innocence. You plot complex strategies of revenge and retaliation. In the end you exhaust yourself and sink into despair. You discover that there is nothing so tiring as entertaining an enemy day after day.

The injured self exists in relationship to an enemy. What is it that makes someone your enemy, apart from your own fear and anger? This is not to suggest that you live in a world of benevolent beings who treasure your well-being, safety, and dignity. There are real situations of harm and abuse, and wisdom requires you to protect yourself and prevent harmful acts. But when you have done all you can do to end the causes of suffering, and you still find yourself dwelling in resentment and hurt, you may begin to sense that it is your own anger and bitterness that have become your enemies. Then you discover how destructive resentment and rage truly are. They poison our lives, destroy our hearts, and leech joy and love from the moment.

The path of compassion asks you to consider what is needed to live with no one as your enemy. The person who harmed you may continue to be aggressive, irritating, exploitative, or hurtful. You may not have the power to change them, but you do have the capacity to liberate yourself from the burden and prison of bitterness. This is a practice of the moment. If you believe that compassion has to wait until you have the ideal life, surrounded by wonderful people with perfect hearts, you will end up postponing life, saving your compassion for the right moment in which to apply it.

I once heard a story about a church service where the pastor was preaching the virtues of forgiveness. He advised the congregation to love their enemies. After sitting for a time with a puzzled look on his face, an old man in the congregation raised his hand. "What if I don't have any enemies so I don't have anyone to forgive?" he asked. Skeptically, the pastor replied, "Are you saying that there is no one who has hurt you, no one you are angry with?" The old man paused for a moment, then answered, "No sir, the bums are all dead." Compassion in the absence of adversity is not difficult;

compassion in the midst of a broken heart asks for profound courage and a commitment to healing all sorrow.

When you live with feelings of hurt born of your interaction with another person, you are invited to explore what compassion means in the absence of good will. Clearly, compassion rises more spontaneously in response to the suffering of those we love, where there is a foundation of affection. We can easily find compassion from a distance for innocent casualties of conflict; we can even find compassion for those who cause pain, if they express remorse and promise to change. The most challenging place to nurture compassion is where the hurt and pain are very personal and good will has vanished.

Rarely do we feel neutral toward our adversaries. Mistrust, fear, and alienation are the residues of hurt. In moments of honesty, you may even recognize that you would like your adversaries to suffer just a little. But you are asked to nurture compassion in the midst of bitterness, hurt, and rejection. If you turn away from doing this, you invite into your heart a foretaste of hell. If you can find the courage and commitment to nurture compassion in the midst of hell, it will be a compassion that is unshakable.

Compassion toward your enemies does not mean that you are obliged to like them or form intimate relationships with them. You may be forever estranged from your adversaries; there may even be wisdom in keeping some distance from them. But none of these acts of discriminating wisdom denies the possibility of compassion. Bowing to your enemies does not mean bowing down to them. Compassion in the face of adversity is not a feeling but a cultivation of wisdom and freedom. You cannot make yourself feel compassionate, but you can, through understanding, empathy, and a refusal to consent to alienation and suffering, incline your heart toward compassion.

Inclining your heart toward compassion begins with a willingness to cultivate calmness amidst the agitation of anger and animosity. The impulse of those powerful emotions is to act—to retaliate outwardly or withdraw into endless repetitions of the story of hurt. Whether you follow the path of punishment and vengeance or sink into the denseness of afflictive emotions and thoughts, you are disconnecting from the simple truth of the suffering of the moment. Agitation camouflages your commitment to heal sorrow, to listen deeply, to open to life. Calmness begins with remembering that commitment. Discovering a trustworthy refuge of stillness in the midst of agitation requires you to be willing to step back from the story line, from injured pride, from the busyness of justification. In the moments of greatest agitation, reclaiming your heart begins with your capacity to connect with that which is not agitated. You can feel your feet on the ground, hear the sound of a bird outside your window, sense the stillness of a tree. Calmness is as close as your next breath.

As you learn to calm and still your heart and mind, you can begin to hear the hurt and fear that underlie the story of bitterness and resentment. This universal story is often the forerunner of the conflict and division that scar our world. It does not ask for further blame; it asks for tenderness. As you heal these scars on a personal level, you heal the world. Transforming the shape of your own mind in the moments of deepest division transforms the shape of the world. Bitterness and resentment unattended to can harden into hatred. Rage cannot be sustained unless it is nourished. Understanding and empathy, when attended to, deepen into compassion. Patience and forgiveness, when nourished, heal suffering.

There is a story of an old rabbi, famous for his wisdom, who came to a village as a guest teacher. The clever young resident rabbi saw this as a wonderful opportunity to show off and prove himself, so he devised a test for the old rabbi. At the right moment, in the middle of the master's speech, the young man determined to approach the elder rabbi with a tiny bird in his hand and say, "Rabbi, I have a bird in my hand. Can you tell me if it is alive or dead?" If the rabbi answered, "The bird is alive," the young man could crush the bird and hold it out for all to see, proving the old man wrong. If the rabbi replied, "The bird is dead," the young man would open his hand and let the bird fly away, demonstrating his superior cleverness and wisdom. The moment came, and the young man approached the rabbi with his question. "Rabbi, you are so learned and wise. Can you tell me if the bird in my hand is alive or dead?" The rabbi was silent for a moment, then with tenderness he looked at the young man and gently replied, "It is up to you, my friend, it is up to you."

In the path of the bodhisattva, patience is said to be one of the noble qualities of heart that is a forerunner of compassion. In the Tao Te Ching, it is written,

> I have just three things to teach:
> simplicity, patience, and compassion.
> These three are your greatest treasures.
> Simple in actions and in thoughts,
> you return to the source of being.
> Patient with both friends and enemies,
> you accord with the way things are.

Compassionate toward yourself,
you reconcile all beings in the world.[1]

Nowhere is patience more needed than in the midst of adversity. Patience is the great healer of mistrust and agitation. You are asked to be patient with your own resentment and bitterness, your rage and fear. If you practice patience in the midst of agitation and animosity, you will, in time, see the end of agitation and animosity.

Patience is not developed in isolation; it is cultivated in all the moments of adversity, large and small, that test the limits of your tolerance and equanimity. Patience is cultivated in your work place, in your family, in the midst of resistance and struggle. Patience is cultivated in the storms of your own heart and mind. Patience is a necessary facet of a life of peace and compassion. It is the quality that allows you to soften, to stay connected, to be intimate in all the moments of adversity you are prone to flee from. Patience is trusting your capacity to bear with the difficult, your capacity to remain steadfast in the face of pain and hurt.

The near enemies of patience are endurance, stoicism, resignation, and despair. All are forms of withdrawal, the surrender of relatedness. William S. Plumer, a Presbyterian minister, teacher, and author, once said, "There is as much difference between genuine patience and sullen endurance as between the smile of love and the malicious gnashing of teeth." Patience is neither submission to abuse or exploitation nor a passive acceptance of suffering or pain. It is an inner steadiness and a commitment to not abandon anyone or anything inwardly or outwardly. The Dalai Lama speaks of patience as the deep ability and willingness to remain firm and steadfast in the face of adversity.

Most of us are not born patient. It is a quality we cultivate, and we rarely lack opportunities to do so. Most of us can recount in endless detail the people and events in the world that we believe are the cause of our impatience and anger. We want life to conform to our image of what ought to happen, and happen according to our timetable, and we feel offended when life fails to measure up. A friend is heartbroken, and you are willing to be present with her suffering for a time. Then you notice impatience arising, perhaps with the thought that she has received her ration of compassion and now she should change. A person you love fails to heed your good advice, and you find yourself annoyed at his continuing problem.

Patience can carry hidden conditions. You want one thing to end and another to begin, and when those conditions remain unmet, you see how much craving and aversion underlie your patience. Compassion asks you to explore how it would be to meet life without conditions or timetables, to meet frustration and adversity without craving or aversion. Patience begins with your willingness to be intimate with frustration and impatience and to turn toward whatever you are prone to abandon. Patience has its roots in the understanding that the source of your impatience is not in the people and situations in your life but in your own heart and mind. Impatience is one of our greatest sufferings; it serves only to mar our capacity to live where we are, to be with what is, and to find peace and stillness in the midst of all things.

Impatience sentences us to the limbo of a life of waiting. We could all write our own life poems of waiting — waiting for adversaries to change, waiting for the current conflict in life to end, waiting for sorrow to be replaced by happiness, waiting for the perfect moment. In that limbo of waiting, the life you want, the life you are willing to live, is always on some distant horizon. A postponed life is a surrender of faith and confidence in yourself. The seeds of compassion lie in your willingness to embrace the life you are living — with all its frustrations and difficulty.

Patience and compassion can be as limitless as the adversity you meet in your life. When the pain of agitation and impatience arise, instead of abandoning them, you can turn toward them with the tenderness you would bring to a child in the throes of a tantrum. *Just this, just now.* Just this one moment asks you to soften and be steadfast. When you sense that something is too much to bear, you begin to understand that it is yet another classroom of patience and compassion.

The kindergarten of patience is in all the small moments where aversion and resistance begin to arise. The person who irritates you, the twinge in your back, the line you must stand in waiting to be served, the monotonous thought that returns to sing its song. These are the moments when you can feel the impulse of abandonment arise. These are the places where you are asked to be steadfast. If there is suffering in these moments that needs courageous and clear action, that is what is called for. If there is suffering that cannot be altered, patience and compassion are called for. Patience is not a magic wand that brings the unpleasant and difficult to an end. It is you who is changed by your willingness to cultivate patience. You learn to not compound the suffering of the moment with aversion and resistance. You withdraw your demand and insistence that the moment be different than it is. It is the beginning of compassion when you are able, even for a moment, to calm the agitation and impatience born of aversion.

You find yourself listening to the cries of the world more willingly.

Adversaries live within your own heart and mind, as does your impatience. The physical, emotional, and psychological events that you meet each day are not always the events you wish for or feel able to welcome. Here too you can find yourself postponing life, rationing your compassion and patience. Learning to find the steadfastness to meet your inner adversaries with calmness is training for meeting all the adversity in life. You think you should be tranquil and enlightened, but sometimes that is just not what is happening. You may be patient for a time and then demand that your patience should produce results. You tell yourself that you are *always* agitated and frustrated and will remain so. *Always* is the great saboteur of patience.

There is a wonderful cartoon by Gahan Wilson in which a young monk has apparently just asked a senior monk a question. The elder monk turns toward his student with a puzzled look on his face and says, "Nothing comes next. This is it." Do you imagine that all the Buddhas and great sages have perfectly calm and tranquil minds, bodies that never trouble them, and lives that are free of adversity? I don't think they do, but they may have profound patience. All of us can cultivate and grow that patience in all the circumstances of life.

Forgiveness will always be part of disarming your enemies, both inwardly and outwardly. Your enemies will remain as thorns in your heart until you begin to find your way toward forgiveness. A Sufi saying declares, "Fear is the cheapest room in the house, and I'd like to see you in better accommodations." Resentment, animosity, and bitterness are the cheapest rooms in the house. Forgiveness is what enables you to move out of those shabby rooms. Are pride and being right more important to you than peace? Is it possible for you to liberate yourself from the injuries of the past?

There are times when it is appropriate to ask forgiveness from those you have harmed through your words and acts. There are also times when you need to forgive those who have harmed you. The absence of forgiveness hinders your recovery. The absence of forgiveness sentences you to a life driven by an unrelenting cycle of resentment and animosity. Forgiveness is evidence of your commitment to release yourself from that cycle and to live your life now, while you have it. Forgiveness is evidence of your commitment to healing the wounds of your world. Compassion is an act of endless forgiveness. Honey J. Rubin once said, "On the wings of forgiveness is carried all other wisdom."

When you explore the places of fear and resentment within your heart, you see that the injured self and the enemy arise simultaneously, bound together in an endless dance. The choreography of the dancers is the endless stream of thoughts and memories of injustice, judgment, blame, and self-righteousness. Beneath it all is fear and hurt. When you visit the injured self, you begin to sense that only you can truly heal the hurt. Even if your enemy apologized endlessly, performed a thousand prostrations at your feet, you would still be left with the task of healing the hurt in your own heart. The hurt you carry is healed not through retaliation or proving your innocence but through compassion. Compassion embraces the pain of a broken heart, knowing this suffering can end.

Forgiveness is a path. You do not forgive just once but countless times in your life. Each time you see yourself recoiling from another person, beginning to walk the pathway of animosity and blame, becoming lost in aversion or resentment, you can feel the pain you are inflicting upon yourself. These are the moments that ask for you to cultivate forgiveness. At the heart of compassion is the commitment to heal the causes of suffering. Alienation, division, belief in the separation between self and other are the greatest causes of suffering in life.

Forgiveness is a gesture of liberation in the service of liberation. Forgiveness liberates you from what has passed, from the burden of resentment and fear. Understanding your enemy may be part of forgiveness. Longfellow once wrote, "If we could read the secret history of our enemies, we should see sorrow and suffering enough to disarm all hostility." You share with your enemies the fear of pain and isolation, the anxiety that leads to armoring, and the capacity to be hurt. You share with your enemies all the confused and deluded activity that can be generated to protect yourself from hurt, which sadly often results in further pain. Understanding your enemies does not excuse their unwholesome or unskillful actions, nor does it diminish the pain you may feel as a result of those actions. Understanding reveals that, as long as any heart is governed by fear and self-cherishing, a trail of hurt and pain will be left in its wake. Forgiveness is an expression of your commitment to not add to the mountain of suffering.

The Buddha taught that hatred is not healed by hatred but by love alone. He also urged us to "live in joy amongst those who hate, in peace amongst those who war, in equanimity amidst those who fear. This is the home of freedom." You may feel that forgiveness is hard, but you pay a much higher price for not forgiving. Forgiveness for yourself and the myriad ways you can harm yourself and others is the embodiment of compassion. Forgiveness for those who have harmed you frees you to live in the present rather than being bound to the past. Forgiveness and compassion go hand in hand. Compassion reconciles all beings in the world.

GUIDED MEDITATION
Compassion in Adversity

Let your body settle into a posture of ease and calmness. Take some moments to listen to the life of your body. If you sense subtle or obvious places of tension or holding in your face, shoulders, abdomen, or anywhere else, allow them to soften. Be aware of the subtle sensations within your body—the movement of your breathing in your chest and abdomen, your heartbeat, and the sensations that arise and pass, moment to moment. Rest a gentle, calm attentiveness in the area of your heart, simply being aware of that area of your body.

Invite into your attention an image of someone you love. Hold that image in your attention and sense the natural warmth and tenderness you feel for the person. Notice the tenderness you feel for one you feel deeply connected with and how beneath that tenderness lies your heartfelt wish for their happiness and well-being. Let your attention rest for some moments in that sense of connectedness that is at the heart of compassion. Be aware also of the sorrow and suffering that is part of that person's life—illness, loss, disappointment, fear, or loneliness. Sense your capacity to meet their sorrow with compassion and offer to that person your deep wish for their well-being and peace.

May you find peace in your heart.
May you find peace in your days.
May you be at peace in all moments.

Let your attention rest in these simple phrases and intentions of compassion for some moments, allowing your sense of connection to deepen. Now begin to open the field of your compassion further, and invite into your attention someone who you struggle with, have been hurt by, or feel alienated from. As much as you are able, picture that person in your mind, and let them rest in your attention. Notice how quickly thoughts about them begin to arise — thoughts of pain, fear, or anger, or memories of your past interactions.

As much as you are able, let the thoughts pass, and hold your attention simply on the image of the person. Notice their face and body, sense their pain and fear. Sense that their pain, fear, and anger is no different than the pain, fear, and anger you have experienced at times in your life. Explore whether it is possible to bring a compassionate heart to bear witness to the sorrow of their suffering. As much as you are able, holding their image in your heart, offer to your adversary your heartfelt wish for their well-being.

May you find peace in your heart.
May you be free from pain and sorrow.
May you find peace in your life.

Holding in your attention the image of the person you feel estranged from, see if it is possible to sense the ways in which they long for love, acceptance, and happiness, just as you do. Sense the confusion and ignorance that lie at the root of their acts and words of harm, destroying their capacity to find the very intimacy and well-being they yearn for. Explore whether it is possible for you to bear witness to their innate longing for love and happiness. Again offer to your adversary your heartfelt wishes that they find ease and well-being in their heart.

> May you find peace.
> May you find healing.
> May you be free from pain and sorrow.

As you embrace the difficult person in your heart, sensing the pain of their life, feel too the power of compassion to heal division and estrangement. Stories of hurt and struggle can be endless. It is possible for you to begin to soften your own fear and hatred. It is possible to change your heart and mind in this moment, to change your world in this moment.

Forgiveness is part of your journey to finding the compassion that can heal. Holding the image of your adversary in your attention, sense the painful feelings of betrayal and hurt that have been caused by the words and acts of that person. Sense the pain of carrying the burden of this past and your longing to be free of that person. As much as you are able, offer forgiveness to the person who has harmed you.

> For the thoughts, words and acts of pain you have inflicted,
>   I forgive you.
> For the harm you have caused, knowingly or unknowingly,
>   I forgive you.

For the sorrow you have caused, I forgive you.
I forgive you.

Gently repeat these phrases. Sense whether it is possible for you to release the burden of pain, resentment, and betrayal. It may be that in repeating the phrases you experience once more the fear and anguish you carry in your heart. Touch this softly with compassion for yourself.

May I be free of pain and sorrow.
May I find peace in my heart.
May I be at peace with all beings.

In learning to touch your adversaries and places of deep anguish within your own heart with compassion, you may need to alternate your attention between the difficult person and yourself. You are learning to bring the simple but powerful compassion and healing to pain. You learn to do this without demand or expectation. Sometimes you are not yet ready to forgive or to connect in your heart with the most difficult people in your life. Your willingness to continue with the contemplation and practice is rooted in your understanding that you are always ready to be free from suffering and its causes.

Compassion and Emptiness 8

THE GREAT SPIRITUAL TRADITIONS liken wisdom and compassion to the two wings of a bird—indivisible and essential to each other. Compassion is not a feeling that can be can manufactured or produced on demand, nor is it a surge of emotion triggered by sorrow and pain. Compassion is a way of being and seeing in the midst of joy and anguish, pleasure and pain, which is deeply rooted in an understanding of emptiness. Compassion is the natural expression and embodiment of a heart without boundaries and a mind unclouded by delusion.

There are two ways of understanding the unfolding of compassion. One is to see compassion as the outcome of a path that can be cultivated and developed. You do not in reality cultivate compassion, but you can cultivate, through investigation, the qualities that incline your heart toward compassion. You can learn to attend to the moments when you close and contract in the face of suffering, anger, fear, or alienation. In those moments, you are asked to question what difference empathy, forgiveness, patience, and tolerance would make. You cultivate the commitment to turn toward your responses of aversion, anger, or intolerance. You are asked to open and embrace not just devastating suffering or tragedy but all the countless small moments where division, mistrust, and fear take root. With mindfulness and investigation, you find in your heart the generosity and understanding that allow you to open rather close.

The willingness to do this is rooted in a mature dissatisfaction with suffering. You are no longer willing to make your home in estrangement and alienation. You see that disconnection, fear, and rage wound yourself and world, and you seek a way beyond them by cultivating patience, generosity, kindness, and intimacy. You are cultivating a climate in which compassion can flourish. It is a training that asks for perseverance and patience.

The second way of understanding compassion is to see it as the natural embodiment of wisdom. Deep insight can reveal the emptiness of all notions of self and other. The world of appearances is no longer mistaken for reality. The Buddha said that emptiness is the abode of the liberated person. Forsaking all notions of duality and separation, compassion becomes the language of emptiness.

The Buddha got up from under the bodhi tree after his awakening declaring, I have done what needs to be done. He did not then withdraw into blissful retirement for the remainder of his life. Enlightenment was not the end of the Buddha's story. Seeing the breadth and the depth of suffering in the world, knowing it had a cause and could end, out of compassion he turned toward the world to offer the path to the end of suffering.

After his enlightenment, the Buddha reentered a world that was essentially unchanged by his awakening. He still had a body that was subject to all the frailties any body experiences. He still had a mind, with all the thoughts, images, and memories of any mind.

He still had an emotional life that could experience sadness and joy. The world was still full of tragedy and beauty, pleasant and unpleasant people, experiences and events he couldn't control. Yet he was changed, his way of being was radically altered. Nowhere did the Buddha counsel denial of this body, mind, or world. Nowhere did he counsel the annihilation or transcendence of life. This is how Nagarjuna, the Indian mystic, described the inter-woven nature of absolute and relative truth:

Life is no different than nirvana
Nirvana no different than life
Life's horizons are nirvana's
The two are exactly the same[1]

For years the Buddha led an engaged and vital life, dedicated to bringing about the end of sorrow. Again and again he taught that there is anguish, there is a cause of anguish, and there is a way to uproot all fear and sorrow. The heart of this path of wisdom is the understanding of emptiness. Emptiness is the garden in which compassion flowers. To understand emptiness is to discover a life of freedom and compassion in the midst of the very real world of events and appearances. The moment we try make even the slight-est separation between freedom and that world, between heaven and hell, between the unconditioned and the conditioned, we fall into an abyss that can only fill with judgment, prejudice, and suf-fering.

Initially the word *emptiness* may strike us as bleak and lifeless. We imagine empty rooms, gaps, a life devoid of vitality and color. We equate emptiness with absence, deprivation. It is a word that can send a tremor of fear through our bodies, as we imagine a life without meaning, direction, or connection. But the great mystics and teachers throughout time have placed the understanding of emptiness at the center of a life of freedom and compassion. Author and scholar Peter Oppenheimer describes emptiness as "perhaps the greatest wealth one can possess, for it provides the arena for adventure, discovery, and creativity."

Emptiness does not describe a dismissal of life but the end of all notions that anything that appears has a fixed and isolated existence, including yourself. Emptiness is not the cessation of life but the cessation of misunderstanding and confusion. The Buddha described emptiness as the wisdom born of uprooting illusion or wrong view. The cause of suffering is not the world with all its change, tragedy, loss, and sorrow. The cause of suffering is the belief that, at the center of this matrix of events, there is an enduring self that is diminished and damaged by what it cannot control. The cause of suffering is the belief in me and mine, you and yours, I and you, and the fixed separation between them. Suffering is born of all the frantic activity of craving and aversion that demonstrates our belief in separation. Defenses are the visible face of our belief in a self. The ongoing encouragement in the teaching of liberation and compassion is to question whether this belief is true.

In the Genjo Koan, Zen master Dogen said, "Meditation is to study the self. To study the self is to forget the self. To forget the self is to be awakened by all things. To be awakened by all things is to let body and mind of self and other fall away."

Throughout his life, the Buddha encouraged his students to take their seats beneath a tree and contemplate, "This is not me, this does not belong to me, this is not who I am." It is a contemplation that goes directly to the heart of all suffering and sorrow, a radical investigation that overturns most of the assumptions that have governed and directed our lives. The liberation of mind through understanding emptiness is the insight that anything that is born and will die is empty of self. .

The story of "me" has been a central one throughout our lives. Consciously and unconsciously, the sense of "I" governs and dictates our responses to all events and experiences we meet. We expend immense energy trying to create a world in which the I feels safe, thereby creating a world of allies and enemies. Once we have arranged the details of our outer world in a way that satisfies the I, we are faced with the endless project of correcting and perfecting our bodies, minds, and hearts so they too are as gratifying as they can be.

The story of I includes the body, feelings, mind, perceptions, and volition. The story of I solidifies around all the events and experiences you have had, creating a past and also a future. You give events, objects, and experiences the power to cause pain pleasure, and in so doing the sense of "other" becomes increasingly solid. The names and concepts you use to define everything in your inner and outer worlds support their independence and solidity. Despite the innumerable changes you have gone through in your life, you approach and interact with the world from the position of an independent and continuous self. Everything outside your body-mind experience is seen as other, which also possesses an independent self-existence.

The belief that the world of the other is separate from yourself is the forerunner of the belief that the other is to be either feared or desired. So begins the life of struggle, whether of pursuit or avoidance. You chase all that you identify as pleasing and flattering — the perfect body, relationship, status, experience — in the belief that their possession will guarantee the enhancement and security of the I. You fear and flee from all that you have decided is threatening — unpleasant people and objects, and experiences of aging, sickness, and death — in the belief that they can shatter the me. This is the world of suffering which has a cause and can have an end.

You are not asked to renounce the world but to release yourself from the tyranny of beliefs that separate you from life and from the freedom and compassion that are possible. You can invite into your heart the investigation, "This is not me, this does not belong to me, this is not who I am." You can begin to sense the liberation and boundlessness born of truly understanding the nature of emptiness. The path of liberation invites you to translate these words into an intuitive and felt understanding. To be empty is to cease being full of self-consciousness. Understanding emptiness does not eliminate the me, but it transforms your way of being present in your life.

If you were to bring these reflections into any moment you experienced today, you might catch a glimmer of the radical transformation they can give birth to. Recall a moment when you felt despairing, angry, or fearful or were experiencing a turbulent mind or painful body. What happens if you consider that experience as belonging to you, as who you are? Perhaps you sense how immediately your heart and mind begin to tighten and contract with the struggle that is born of those beliefs. Now sense what happens if you consider that same experience as not you, not yours, not who you are. The world of blame, fear, and struggle falls away, as identification falls away. It doesn't mean that your back stops aching or your mind stops thinking. It doesn't mean that you stop caring or responding to all that asks for your care and response. But it can mean that you cease to struggle and suffer. Understanding emptiness is an open door to a life of participation, born of a heart that no longer sets itself apart from life.

Intellectually, it is not difficult to understand emptiness. If you sat down and looked at photographs of yourself throughout your life, it would be apparent that who you believe yourself to be today is different from the you of five, ten, or twenty years ago. You can trace through those images your metamorphosis from infant, to child, to teenager and identify the various roles you have assumed at different stages in your life. You will remember, perhaps with some embarrassment, the certainties and opinions that came with those identities. As a political radical, a flower child, or an aspiring president, you were convinced that your views and identity were eternal.

How you see yourself in this moment may be entirely different than your experience of yourself yesterday or even a few hours ago. The discontented self who turned up for breakfast may have been replaced by the enthusiastic, hopeful self who appeared at lunch, only to morph into the weary, doubtful self at dinner. The conditions of your mind, body, heart, and life are in a constant state of flux. You heroically endeavor to find stability and make life stand still by clinging to anything that enhances and by resisting anything that threatens you. You say, "This is me, this belongs to me, this is who I am." But within the unfolding matrix of conditions of the moment, there is nothing that has an independent existence. Without the storyteller there is no story; without the story, no storyteller. Without an I, there is no you; without a you, there is no

I. The thinker and the thought arise and fall together. The sound and the listener, the sorrow and the sufferer, the experience and the experiencer, all arise and fall together.

Within this changing flow of conditions and events, nothing stands still, nothing possesses an independent existence, nothing remains static. There is nothing we can call me or mine. In the teaching of the Buddha, this understanding — direct, experiential, and profound — is called the understanding of emptiness. In the years after the Buddha's death, long before the advent of images and statues, he was most often depicted in images of emptiness — a set of footprints in sand, a vacant hut, an empty seat beneath a tree.

Everything single thing you can see, feel, touch, and experience has a lineage of conditions, the beginning of which will always be untraceable. The paper these words are printed on is just a momentary expression of a combination of conditions — trees, paper mills, workers, earth, sun, seeds. Each component in that lineage has its own lineage. You could contemplate a flower and see its timelessness. If you dismantled the flower, you would hold in your hands a leaf, a stem, a petal — none of which in themselves could be called a rose, yet together forming a rose. Your body in this moment is born of countless conditions, so too your mind, your emotions, your thoughts, opinions, and perceptions.

Everything you experience and think in this moment is part of a new lineage, which you call the future. This moment is the parent of the next moment. Reflecting on the changing conditions of life, you can begin to sense that there is no true beginning or end. Everything arises from and falls back into an unbroken stream of conditions. When you can forsake, even a little, the endless and futile attempts to make life stand still, you begin to find just a little more ease in your life. When you can begin to let go, even a little, of the belief that this is me, belongs to me, is who I am, you begin to discover a greater sense of freedom. Contemplating life and beginning to see that everything you encounter is neither intrinsically desirable nor fearful, you can to step out of the perpetual cycle of pursuit and avoidance. You are able to open to each moment just as it is, rather than being lost in the appearance of things.

Understanding emptiness does not dismiss or diminish the very real joy and tragedy in the world. It is not a rejection of the world of appearances. Understanding emptiness frees you to participate and cooperate in the world with compassion and love. Hui Neng, a great Chinese teacher, said, "Emptiness includes the sun, moon, stars, and planets, the great earth, mountains and rivers, all trees and grasses, bad men and good men, bad things and good things, heaven and hell, they are all in the midst of emptiness.[2]"

Understanding emptiness does not mean divorcing yourself from or disdaining the world of appearances. Instead it opens your heart to the sorrow, struggle, and vulnerability of all beings. Out of that openness is born the longing to relieve suffering. From the wisdom of emptiness is born compassion.

Meditation inevitably begins with the contemplation of the self. No matter how great your altruism or how lofty the ideals you seek to accomplish in your meditation, the reality is that when you sit down on a cushion you meet your self. Spending just fifteen minutes alone with yourself in silence offers a cameo of the self-consciousness that is so central to our lives. You meet the body of your self, with all its discomforts, complaints, and places of ease. Your first response is usually, *This is me, it's happening to me, it's who I am.* If the feeling in the body is unpleasant, you squirm, flinch, and recoil. You might find yourself beginning to strategize a way out of the pain or even blaming yourself for it. A pleasant experience may generate a different set of responses, as you search for ways to maintain it.

If, with patience, you are able to be still and study what is actually occurring in your body, you will begin to understand more deeply the life of the body. Sensations emerge and fade away. Beneath the concepts of "my knee," "my back" is a world of changing sensations devoid of solidity and permanence. You may begin to find the equanimity and patience that frees you from the frantic reactions of avoidance or pursuit. Nothing in your body is constant or eternal. Listening to the life of your body, you may begin to experientially understand that it is not you and does not belong to you. This understanding is not disabling; if there is suffering in the body, you reach out to tend to it with care and compassion. In contemplating your body, you are in truth contemplating all bodies, all born of conditions and fading away to be part of a new matrix and appearance. Bodies are born and die. Bodies experience pain and suffering. To understand this is to understand that there is no alternative but compassion. As Shantideva said:

> Just as these arms and legs
> Are seen as limbs of a body.
> Why are embodied beings
> Not seen as limbs of life.[3]

Sitting quietly, you also meet the mind of your self—the cascade of thoughts, images, memories, fantasies, plans, and concepts that are part of your life in every moment. Sometimes you find yourself lost in thoughts, at other times you try to control them or push them away. There are moments when you unconsciously or consciously entertain yourself with your thoughts. Initially, the mind seems to be deeply interesting, until you study it closely.

Studying the life of the mind, you see that the vast majority of your mental activities are simply superfluous. At times they are no more than activities of agitation and anxiety, filling your consciousness to the extent that deep stillness and listening are denied. You try to stop thinking and discover that it only creates tension. You try to patient, believing that eventually your thoughts will exhaust themselves, only to discover that this is not so. The attempt to control your thoughts or indulge in them both betray the belief that your thoughts are you, are who you are, and that they do in truth belong to you. On reflection, it is clear that you did not wake this morning and decide it was a good day to be irritable or obsessive. Nor can you wake in the morning and determine that today you will only have positive, uplifting thoughts. Thoughts emerge and fall away. Freed from the activities of aversion, agitation, or identification, the activities of mind are no obstacle to stillness or compassion. The obstacle lies in holding to and identifying with the waves of activity in the mind. By studying mind, you loosen the ties of identification with it.

When a thought arises, if it is not dwelt upon, pursued, or resisted, it will simply fall away. As mindful awareness deepens, you discover a stillness within that embraces all the movements and waves of mind. The inclination to cling, obsess, or become agitated falls away. You discover a calm, acutely receptive and sensitive space that is deeply responsive and sensitive to everything that appears, yet is not lost in anything. The tendency to isolate any thought, feeling, image, or perception into a fixed and solid entity begins to fade away. The inclination to lay claim to any of the arising and passing events in the mind and name them as "me" or "mine" loses strength. Experientially and directly, you see the suffering and isolation born of such claims, so letting go is intuitive and immediate. The disinclination to identify or fix anything in this world, inwardly or outwardly, does not imply an absence of responsibility; instead it liberates you to participate fully in this life with wisdom and compassion.

You sit silently in meditation to study the self, only to discover it is exceedingly difficult to find a self to study. What you find yourself studying instead is the appearance of self, as a sense of "me" isolates and tries to fix events that arise and pass in the body, mind, and world. Trying to find the self is like trying to pin down your shadow. It is ephemeral, in a constant state of change, impervious to your attempts to make it stand still. Sometimes you find yourself believing that it is the self that causes suffering, so you engage in heroic efforts to subdue, transcend, or perfect the self. You adopt a new belief that you must annihilate the self in order to be free. You see liberation and an understanding of emptiness as a different dimension, separate from the world of appearance. Once more you have created separation, dividing heaven and hell, this world and another world, and once more you suffer. Dogen described the interrelatedness of emptiness and the world of appearance, saying:

Enlightenment is like the moon reflected on the water. The moon doesn't get wet and the water isn't broken. Although its light is broad and great, the moon is reflected even in a puddle an inch wide. The whole moon and sky are reflected even in one dewdrop on the grass. Enlightenment doesn't destroy the person, just as the dewdrop doesn't hinder the moon in the sky.[4]

Just as you see that the self has no independent, fixed reality, you also see that it is not nothing. Each of us brings our own unique memories, experiences, and past to life. Your body, the way you respond, think, and perceive are to some extent unique to you. Your history, hopes, dreams, and fears differ even from those of your loved ones. They are the building blocks of your story. Liberation does not ask you to erase or deny your story but to understand deeply where there is suffering and delusion within it. In the midst of your story, you learn to find the way to the end of suffering and delusion. You explore where there is entanglement and where there is freedom.

The wisdom and compassion you most deeply yearn for will not be found outside of your body, mind, heart, or story but within them. Understanding their nature deeply, you come to understand the nature of all bodies, minds, and hearts. Learning to heal the sorrow and anguish within yourself, you learn the lessons of healing all sorrow and anguish. Learning to meet every moment of suffering and pain in your life with compassion and wisdom, you find the vastness of genuine compassion that embraces all suffering. The notions of me and you, self and other, dissolve in the depths of a profound understanding of emptiness. What remains is compassion, immeasurable and vast. As Chuang Tzu taught:

Do not seek fame, do not be a storehouse of schemes, do not be an undertaker of projects, do not be an owner of wisdom. Embody to the fullest what has no end and wander where there is no trail. Hold on to all that you have received from heaven but do not think that you have gotten anything. Be empty, that is all.

GUIDED MEDITATION
Compassion without Boundaries

Settle into a calm and centered posture. Breathe gently and sense the life of your body, mind, and heart in this moment. Sense your own yearning for peace, safety, and well-being. Feel too the way you defend against sorrow and pain. Invite into your attention someone you care for, sensing the sorrows in their life, and their longing for happiness, peace, and well-being. Notice how your heart can open to embrace those you care for, feeling their sorrow and responding with a natural compassion. Offer to yourself, to the one you love, the articulated intentions of compassion.

May I find healing and peace.
May you find healing and peace.

Let your attention rest gently in these phrases for a time, and then allow the range of your attention and compassion to expand. Sense the countless beings in this world who in this moment have their own measure of anguish, their own longings for peace and healing. Imagine yourself seated in the center of a mandala, surrounded by the innumerable beings who at this moment are hungry, bereft, afraid, or in pain. Imagine yourself breathing in that immeasurable pain, the sorrow and the ignorance that causes sorrow. With each out breath, sense yourself breathing out unconditional compassion.

> May all beings find healing.
> May all beings find peace.
> May all beings be held in compassion.

Allow yourself to sense the countless beings in the world who are ill or dying, who are grieving, who are lonely and estranged. Embrace in your attention those who are imprisoned and those who imprison, those who are caught in the terrors of war and violence and those who war and inflict violence. Without reservation enfold all beings in a heart of compassion.

> May all beings be free from sorrow.
> May all beings be free from suffering.
> May all beings be free.

Let your heart fill with the compassion possible for all of us, the compassion that listens deeply to the cries of the world.

Notes

Introduction

1. Stephen R. Harrison, *Whispered Prayers* (Santa Barbara, Calif.: Talisman Press, 2000), 127.

Chapter 2

1. Pablo Neruda, "Keeping Quiet." in *Extravagaria*, trans. Alastair Reid (New York: Farrar, Strauss and Giroux, 1994).

Chapter 3

1. Christina Feldman and Jack Kornfield, eds., *Soul Food* (San Francisco: Harper San Francisco, 1996), 252.

Chapter 5

1. Kabir "Difficulties," in *The Soul Is Here for Its Own Good*, ed. Robert Bly (Hopewell, N.J.: The Ecco Press, 1995), 72.
2. Quoted in Josh Baron, *365 Nirvana* (London: Element, 2003), 49.

Chapter 7

1. Quoted in Stephen Mitchell, *Enlightened Heart* (New York: Harper and Row, 1989), 17.

Chapter 8

1. Quoted in Stephen Batchelor, *Verses from the Center* (New York: Riverhead, 2000), 51.
2. Ibid., 28.
3. Ibid., 32.
4. Quoted in Stephen Mitchell, *Enlightened Mind* (New York: HarperCollins, 1991), 97.

Appreciations

About the Author

IN THE EARLY 1970S, Christina Feldman spent several years in Asia, studying and training in the Buddhist meditation tradition. She has led insight mediation retreats in the West since 1974. A cofounder of Gaia House, in Devon, England, she is a regular teacher at the Insight Meditation Society in Barre, Massachusetts, and at Spirit Rock, in Woodacre, California. In addition, she leads retreats in Europe.

She is the coauthor (with Jack Kornfield) of Soul Food, and the author of Quest of the Warrior Woman, Ways of Meditation, and Buddhist Path to Simplicity, as well as Silence, Woman Awake, and Compassion (all published by Rodmell Press). She lives in Totnes, Devon, England.

For more information, visit www.gaiahouse.co.uk.

From the Publisher

SHAMBHALA PUBLICATIONS is pleased to publish the Rodmell Press collection of books on yoga, Buddhism, and aikido. As was the aspiration of the founders of Rodmell Press, it is our hope that these books will help individuals develop a more skillful practice—one that brings peace to their daily lives and to the Earth.

To learn more, please visit www.shambhala.com.

Index

body
  being embodied versus tran-
    scending, 94
  being mindful of, 95–96
  Buddha's, 142
  communication by, 96–97
  compassion for yours, 92–93,
    94–99
  constant change in, 147, 150
  contemplation in meditation, 95
  dismissal and neglect in spiritual
    paths, 94
  embodying understandings, 98
  heart and mind mirrored in, 97
  identification with, 95, 98
  illness in, 96, 97–98
  lessons learned in, 98–99
  meeting in meditation, 149–150
  microcosmic view of relation-
    ships in, 83
  negative views of one's own, 85
  nonharming and, 99
  pain during meditation, 96
  seasons of, 95
  seen as other, 96
  wisdom and compassion found
    within, 153
breast cancer, 97–98
Buddha
  on the body, 98
  on clear intention, 77
  on clinging, 115
  compassion embodied by, 13
  on compassion for oneself, 83
  contemplation encouraged by,
    144–145, 146
  on emptiness, 142, 148
  on healing hatred, 136
  on the mind, 102
  on practice of compassion,
    90–91

reentry into the world, 142–143
  responsibility felt by, 57
  on shape of your mind, 124–125
  view of the body, 94
Buddhism. See also bodhisattva vow
  central place of compassion in, 7
  meditative training for compas-
    sion in, 53
  Tibetan community in exile, 61
busyness, 22

caring, nonattachment and, 26
Cha, Aachan, 112
change
  embracing, 111–112, 117
  fear of, 111
  inner and outer, 117
  law of, 24
  loss brought by, 24–25
  refusal to accept, 25
  in sense of self, 31, 147–148,
    150, 152
  story of I and, 147–148
  universality of disappearance,
    110–111
character of compassion, 15
children
  abuse of, healing, 75–76
  depression in, 20
  overcoming prejudice in, 35–36
  parents' emotions reflected in,
    109–110
  in Sisters of Charity nursery, 39
Christ, compassion embodied by,
    13
Chuang Tzu, 153–154
clinging. See attachment
Cohen, Leonard, 92
commitment. See also resolve
  to awakening, 48
  to being present, 22–23

dying, trying to do it "right," 84–85

embodying compassion, 12–13
empathy
　as basis of compassion, 51–52
　compassion as ability for, 19
　compassion as force of, 4
　defined, 52–53
　as vulnerability, 54
emptiness
　as abode of liberated person, 142
　compassion as language of, 142
　conditions and, 148–149
　as end of isolation, 144
　as garden where compassion
　　flowers, 143
　as greatest wealth, 144
　guided meditation, 154–155
　heart opened by, 149
　not absence or deprivation,
　　143–144
　studying the self and, 152
　understanding of, 145, 146,
　　147, 148–149
　world of appearance and,
　　152–153
endurance
　as enemy of patience, 131
　tolerance versus, 76–77
enemies. See also adversity
　cultivating calmness amidst, 129
　disarming with forgiveness,
　　134–135
　injured self bound to, 135
　living without, 127
　made by fear and anger, 126–127
　nurturing compassion toward,
　　128–129
　Shantideva on, 71
　suffering shared with, 136

enlightenment. See also liberation
　commitment to awakening, 48
　Dogen on, 152–153
　trying to be worthy of, 85
equanimity
　amidst small transgressions, 72
　meditation as training in, 72–73
　meeting your demons and, 73
　nurturing within, 70
　violence and, 76
escape mechanisms, 20
expectations
　commitment undermined by,
　　45–46
　despair as price of, 42–43
　willingness to let go, 43

faith, fear as denial of, 125
fear. See also anxiety
　acceptance of yours, 12
　body and, 95, 96, 98, 99
　of change, 111
　commitment not to be governed
　　by, 51
　crossing the border of, 74
　cultural propagation of, 68–69
　denial as expression of, 116–117
　as denial of faith, 125
　of disappointment, 27
　embracing, 65
　enemies made by, 126–127, 135
　Gandhi on, 65
　in guided meditation practice, 59
　hope as door to, 45
　of intimacy with pain, 34
　isolation from, 30, 31, 32–33
　as lifelong condition, 11–12
　looking within for causes, 15
　of loss, 111, 112
　as obstacle to compassion, 10–11
　as offspring of separation, 69

overcoming at death, 84–85
pity as face of, 50
resistance and rage governed
by, 63
seeking the way beyond, 142
self-improvement and, 11
separation and, 113
of suffering, 17
tolerance obstructed by, 71
understanding versus reacting
and, 36
Feldman, Christina, 161
forgiveness
asking for, 135
child abuse and, 75–76
compassion as choosing, 36
disarming enemies with,
134–135
as embodiment of compassion,
136–137
as gesture of liberation, 136
healing and, 135
for oneself, 136
as a path, 135–136
for personal failures, 27–28
restorative justice and, 76
understanding needed for, 68
for your own pain and sorrow,
83–84
foundations of compassion,
51–52, 70

Gandhi, 65
Genjo Koan, 144
Geshe Rapden, 55
gratitude, reflecting on, 55
grief
beneath pain, 24–25
body and, 96
honest, 49
personal failures and, 27–28

refusal to accept life and, 25
guided meditations
compassion for ourselves,
104–106
compassion for the blameless,
57–59
compassion for those we love,
119–122
compassion for those who cause
suffering, 79–82
compassion in adversity,
137–140
compassion without boundaries,
154–155
guilt, healing not born out of, 56

happiness
externalizing, 28–29
interdependence and, 31–32
hatred. See also anger
Buddha on healing, 136
Gandhi on, 65
peace prohibited by, 66, 126
poisoning by, 64
psychology of, 63
healing
acceptance of suffering and, 20
bitterness and resentment,
129–130
commitment to, 48–49
commitment to being present
and, 22–23
compassion and love as, 52
compassion as invitation to, 55
embracing your limits, 108
forgiveness and, 135
found in stillness, 41
as gift of compassion, 8
good acts versus, 56
Milarepa on, 16
not born of revenge, 126

interdependence versus isolation,
31–32
intimacy. *See also* compassion for
those we love
body and, 94
as forerunner of acceptance, 92
as key to compassion, 95
patience and, 132
intolerance. *See* tolerance
isolation. *See also* alienation;
disconnection; self and other;
separation
choosing compassion over, 64
compassion not cultivated in, 3
crossing the abyss of, 32–33
defined, 30
emptiness as end of, 144
fragility of, 3
identification and, 31–32
interdependence versus, 31–32
pain of, 30–33
patience not developed in, 131
prejudice and, 32
as price of indifference, 41
turning toward sorrow and shed-
ding of, 23–24
as worst punishment, 53

judgment. *See also* blame; prejudice;
self-judgment
acceptance of yours, 10–11
discrimination and, 90
diving beneath, 32–33
as lifelong condition, 11–12
separation and, 143
of society, 19
understanding versus reacting
and, 36

Kabir, 86–87
Keller, Helen, 4

Kuan Yin, 7, 13–14

law of change, 24
letting go
being present and, 114
of clinging, 115
of illusions about love, 112
life as ongoing teaching in, 110
loss of loved ones and, 116
peace found by, 112
as process, not destination, 113
of self-judgment, 88
of what "should be," 114–115
wisdom of, 25
Levine, Stephen, 24
liberation. *See also* enlightenment
Buddha's reentry into the world
after, 142–143
commitment to awakening, 48
emptiness as abode, 142
forgiveness and, 136
story of I and, 153
through understanding emptiness, 145
listening to the cries of the world
awareness and, 33
being part of the world, 93
being still and, 23
busyness as defense against, 22
calming the agitation of aversion
and, 133–134
compassion for ourselves and, 93
crossing the divide that separates, 9, 32–33
meaning of Kuan Yin and, 7
as path of compassion, 9
prejudices as obstacles to, 10–11
responsibility to respond, 55
loss
from disillusionment, 27
fear of, 111, 112

treating as failure, 96
vast fabric of, 39–40
from wanting, 29
yours, compassion for, 83–84
paradigm of compassion, 15
passivity
acceptance versus, 119
compassion versus, 77
path of compassion
cultivation of, 141–142
listening to the cries of the world
as, 9
mindfulness and, 56–57
wisdom as, 142–143
patience
in adversity, 131–134
"always" as saboteur of, 134
in bodhisattva path, 130
defined, 131
enemies of, 131
as foundation of compassion, 70,
78, 130
hidden conditions for, 132
learning in small moments,
133–134
loved ones' pain and, 108
meditation as training in, 72–73
separation removed by, 74
toward emotions, 103
for your own pain and sorrow,
83–84
peace
acceptance as beginning of, 119
letting go and, 112
prohibited by hatred, 30, 126
with what is, 30
perfection
equating compassion with, 85
idealized notions of, 11
as motivation for spiritual
life, 85

seeking self-perfection, 85–87
"should" and, 87
personal experiences, universal
nature of, 14
pity
compassion versus, 50–51
self-pity, 91
Plumer, William S., 131
postponing compassion, avoiding,
11
prayer, true, 88
prejudice. See also judgment
alienation and, 75
crossing the border of, 74
isolation and, 32
looking within for causes, 14–15
meeting the demon of, 73
as obstacle to compassion, 10
overcoming in children, 35–36
separation and, 143
understanding versus reacting
and, 36
protection
connectedness versus, 125
examining mechanisms of,
69–70
impossibility of, 41
seeking from suffering, 20–21
psychology of hatred, 63–64
punishment, 129

qualities of compassion, 15

rage. See anger; hatred
Ram Dass, 103
realism, altruism and, 69–70
reassurance, 45
resentment. See also anger
blame and, 66
commitment to healing and, 48
difficulty of living with, 5

dwelling in, 127
forgiveness and moving beyond,
134–135
grief beneath, 24
hurt and fear underlying, 129
mind shaped by, 125
as obstacle to compassion,
10–11
poisoning by, 127
stillness in midst of, 72
resignation, 131
resilience, acceptance of pain and,
46–47
resistance
acceptance of yours, 10–11
crossing the border of, 74
governed by fear, 63
in guided meditation practice,
59
learning to soften, 115–116,
117–118
as lifelong condition, 11–12
to loss, 113
meeting the demon of, 73
to memories of harm, 125–126
to personal failures, 28
pity as face of, 50
selective awareness as, 35
to suffering, 17
resolve. See also commitment
as antidote to despair, 47
as bridge to world, 64
to end suffering, 47–48, 77
to path between anger and
despair, 49
renewed again and again, 48
respect, 51
responsibility
of the Buddha, 57
for every action, 56–57
mindfulness and, 56–57

motivations for meditation
and, 54
to participate in healing, 55
personal, compassion versus, 56
to respond to the cries of the
world, 55
revenge
disconnection and, 129
healing not born of, 126
Rodmell Press, 163
romanticism, avoiding, 2
Rubin, Honey J., 135

sainthood, 85
self and other. See also alienation;
disconnection; isolation; separation
body seen as other, 96
crossing the divide between, 9,
32–33, 103, 113
defined by what you possess, 69
dualism challenged by compassion, 84
falling away of, 144, 153
fear and desire springing from,
145–146
isolation and, 31
story of I and, 145
self, compassion for. See compassion for ourselves
self-blame. See self-judgment
self-improvement
not postponing compassion
for, 11
tyranny of seeking self-
perfection, 85–87
self-judgment
baggage coming with, 90
beliefs underlying, 89
difficulty of letting go of, 88
embracing suffering and, 87–88